SURRENDER

Don Baunsgard

ISBN 979-8-89309-562-3 (Paperback)
ISBN 979-8-89309-563-0 (Digital)

Copyright © 2024 Don Baunsgard
All rights reserved
First Edition

All rights reserved. No part of this publication may be reproduced, distributed, or transmitted in any form or by any means, including photocopying, recording, or other electronic or mechanical methods without the prior written permission of the publisher. For permission requests, solicit the publisher via the address below.

Covenant Books
11661 Hwy 707
Murrells Inlet, SC 29576
www.covenantbooks.com

CONTENTS

The Awakening
Chapter 1   The Red Pill 5
Chapter 2   Unashamed 21
Chapter 3   Crashing through Existence 40
Chapter 4   Pew Warmer 55
Chapter 5   Lose so You Can Win 68
Chapter 6   Who Am I? 81
Chapter 7   Predestined 99

The Surrendering
Chapter 8   Heart of Stone 115
Chapter 9   Chosen 133
Chapter 10   Jesus Freak 147
Chapter 11   Sacrifice 163
Chapter 12   Endgame 177
Chapter 13   Genuine Repentance 195
Chapter 14   I Surrender 208

THE AWAKENING

So, my Christian friend, if you are settling back, snuggling into your foam rubber chair and resting in your faith in John 3:16 and the fact that you have accepted Jesus Christ, you had better watch yourself. Take heed, lest you also be found wanting. Take heed of your own heart, lest when all is said and done, you have become tied in with the world.

—A. W. Tozer, *The Dangers of a Shallow Faith: Awakening from Spiritual Lethargy*

Mediocre Christianity

Read your New Testament again and you will agree that mediocrity in the Christian life is not the highest that Jesus offers. Certainly, God is not honored by our arrested spiritual development—our permanent half-way spiritual condition. We all know that the Bible tells us that we honor God by going on to full maturity in Christ! Why, then, do we settle for those little pleasures that tickle the saintliest and charm the fancy of the carnal?

It is because we once heard a call to take up the cross and instead of following towards the heights, we bargained with the Lord like a street huckster! We felt an urge to be spent for Christ, but instead of going on, we started asking questions. We begin to bicker and bargain with God about His standards for spiritual attainment. This is plain truth—not about unbelieving Liberals—but about those who have been born again and who dare to ask, "Lord, what will it cost me?" (A. W. Tozer)

CHAPTER 1

The Red Pill

God has a plan for your life. The enemy has a plan for your life. Be ready for both. Be wise enough to know which one to battle and which one to embrace.
—TobyMac, *Speak Life*

Being a Christian is less about cautiously avoiding sin than about courageously and actively doing God's will.
—Dietrich Bonhoeffer

No one foresaw the magnitude of the movie of which I'm about to quote. In fact, it is totally cliché to even speak of or quote from it. Okay, maybe some foresaw the brilliance, but I admit, I never saw it coming.

All I must do is quote a couple sentences and you will know the movie I am about to reference. And if you haven't seen it, I will explain it as best as I can.

So here you go or more accurately, here *we* go!

> This is your last chance. After this, there is no turning back. You take the blue pill—the story ends, you wake up in your bed and you believe whatever you want to believe. You take the red

> pill—you stay in Wonderland, and I show you
> how deep the rabbit hole goes. (Morpheus)

Am I right? Not such a difficult task if you are a movie buff like me. Even those who may not watch a lot of movies can either remember or guess, with fair accuracy, that this is of course, *The Matrix*.

The quote I just mentioned is profound, and for those who haven't seen it, let me explain.

In the movie, Morpheus, who is in the real world, which is basically underground because the world they once knew has been destroyed by the Matrix, has been looking for Neo, who is in the Matrix, and is currently also in a dream sleep hooked up to tubes all over his body which are withdrawing electricity from him and a million others to feed into the Matrix so it can continue to run. Morpheus has been looking for Neo because he believes he is the One who will free them from bondage and destroy the Artificial Intelligence, otherwise known as the Matrix.

Once he found him, he was on track to open his mind to the reality of the Matrix. But before I can explain the Matrix, let me dive a little deeper and give you the prequel to the main theme of the movie. In the year 2199, the humans and AI had a falling out. AI eventually saw humans as a threat to their existence and took over the world with force. With humans literally plugged into the Matrix, basically slaves to the Matrix, AI could tap into the bioelectricity that the human body produces. Therefore, humans are used as a source of electrical and heat energy by the machines of the Matrix. From babies to adults, the humans are plugged into the Matrix and don't know or realize that they are kept in a state of simulated dream sleep which will take place over their entire lives all the while believing that they are living out normal lives as they sleep.

Neo senses the truth about the Matrix and is seeking out a way to find the truth so he can break free from the Matrix. Morpheus locates Neo, pulls him out of the Matrix, and offers him the red pill or the blue pill which, as I quoted above and according to which pill he takes, will either (red pill) reveal to him the entire truth of his existence, or if he takes the blue pill, he can continue to be plugged into the Matrix and live out a false life believing whatever he wants without any fault or reprimand.

I remember when many moons ago, I had heard that my pastor was going to do a sermon series on *The Matrix* and the deep material hidden within its meanings, symbolism, and twisted theology. But is it really that twisted? How much underlying truth is hidden within this movie that, even now, the main theme of the movie can easily resonate within today's hot topics, social media tactics, political persuasions, and sheer obvious evil that has been crafted to transparently dominate our world, manipulate our lives, and vehemently try and shine its dark light so bright for all to see?

We are living in a time of absolute evil, and it is in our face for all to see. I cannot think of another time since I have been on this planet with the likes of what is happening all over our world to not question the series of events and ask, "What the heck is going on?"

This book you now hold in your hand is on a mission to dive into these current events and hopefully bring to the surface and shine some light on the evil worming its way through our world. We will look at some of the craziness and nonsense that doesn't make any sense, so we can analyze it, question it, and hopefully come to some form of understanding. While we are deciphering the nonsense of our world, I would also like to put forth a challenge to you, the reader, to also bring to the surface some biblical truth in the pursuit of knowing Jesus and choosing to truly follow the Rabbi. Am I truly living my life for Jesus, or am I stuck in the Matrix?

It is my intention to speak as clearly and as humbly as I can with whatever and wherever the Holy Spirit leads me. It is always my hope and prayer that the love and light of Christ shines through so brightly that you are overcome with tears of joy and a heart overflowing with biblical truth. I am hoping this book will be a journey filled with adventure, surprises, and fun, but that it will also contain subjects that will be slightly uncomfortable and difficult to hear, but always with the intention of helping those who need to hear it so they may grow and become more like our Savior, Jesus Christ. Are you ready?

Let's begin.

Today, October 2, 2023, is the day I started writing this book. The only reason I am adding the date of this book is to have reference with what is or has already happened in this timeframe of our history.

Just so most of you know, writing a book is an odd thing. I never know where I am going with the subject matter or how I am going to start or how it is going to end. I just let it flow and see what sticks to the wall. Sometimes, in the editing phase, I will delete whole chapters simply because they did not fit within the parameters of the rest of the book. I have had to do that twice. And it is awkward, but I believe it is absolutely necessary to the overarching message of the book and its fluidity.

Life can happen in the same way. In fact, there are many chapters throughout my life that I would gladly delete if I could and pretend they never happened. But just like writing a book, they are necessary in the creation process. Life sometimes gives us moments of clarity through disappointment, poor choices, pain, and discomfort. These I like to call life markers leave a mark to guide us (hopefully) in the right direction. Or at least to help us see more clearly who we once were and would rather not want to be again.

In the process of writing my life story through the three books I have already written, people have often mentioned how I have shared the transparency of my faults, my sins, and my poor choices. This seems to be the one common factor that people resonate with. They often want to share with me how much they appreciated my willingness to be so open and transparent about my poor choices and the vulnerability it took to share that with the world.

In this, we are most definitely in the same boat, all rowing in circles with a broken oar, trying to figure out where the heck we are going and how to fix our mistakes.

It has been brought to my attention the true importance of needing to hear each other's stories. Not so we can make ourselves feel better about who we are, not to play the victim or to try and outshine somebody else with a more drastic horror story, but to come to the realization that we need to know each other better and therefore understand each other with more compassion, grace, and patience.

SURRENDER

The enemy tends to keep us wallowing in shame and guilt over our past broken and destructive choices to where we struggle to admit and acknowledge where we have gone wrong. When we bring those faults out into the light, he can no longer control us!

This has become the staple to which people can relate and step into my story with a full perspective of how far I have had to come to be the man I am today. Not for my glory but to bring glory to God. Through my pain, through my struggles, God took this broken man, sinful, wretched man, and spoke to me, chose me to bring forth and fulfill the plan and purpose for which I was created. And through this man's pain, to show the world that he can be useful to fulfill God's glorious greater plan and fulfill prayers that needed to be answered.

This book is just one more step in that direction. I can only pray, trust, and have faith that God once more has a plan for these words on paper. Someone needs to read this. Someone out there needs to hear these words and then, hopefully, apply them to their lives. Someone needs to be awakened and shown the truth of the Matrix of this world.

I have always loved the analogy that iron sharpens iron. We cannot do this thing called life alone. We *need* each other. And with that truth, I want to take this moment to offer you the red pill or the blue pill. I am hoping to awaken your mind and reveal the truth that is being hidden or blocked by the world that wants to keep us in darkness, wants to keep us asleep so we won't see clearly the evil flowing waist-deep all around us. If you so choose, I am hoping you will take the red pill and let me show you how deep the rabbit hole goes.

> For the Spirit God gave us does not make us timid, but gives us power, love and self-discipline. (Paul, 2 Timothy 1:7)

Many times, on your daily walk, God is moving powerfully behind the scenes. There may be moments, coincidences, and challenges that pop up out of nowhere and these are planned by God for you to hear and grow in your faith. Or it is a moment of rebuke and discipline. Or it is simply Satan tempting you and trying to knock you off your path. These are all moments for discernment, truth-seeking, heart-wrenching, soul-twisting opportunities to refine you through fire.

I *love* these moments, but I also despise them because they are hard. However, they are necessary in the pursuit of Christ and his will for your life. Honestly, if it was easy to follow Christ, if it was easy to pick up our cross daily and follow him, everyone would do it. But it is just the opposite. And with that, we begin our journey. I do not believe that it is an accident that you are reading this book right now at this very moment. There is something, or many things, that God wants to say to you. And if there is one thing that I now know, it is that God speaks to us through many ways and through many different avenues. Our job is to make sure we are tuned in to his station. If you are not tuned in, you will not hear him. At least, this is my experience.

In the movie *The Matrix*, one key figure is a woman named Trinity. And what a coincidence that her name should be Trinity! (Side note: I named my daughter Trinity because I loved it the first time I heard it.)

Anyway, Trinity is a key source to Neo on his transition from the Matrix into the real world as she works side by side with Morpheus to release Neo from being plugged into the Matrix, but also to help Neo realize that he is the One who will destroy the Matrix and AI and free everyone who is trapped in the Matrix and bring them back into the real world.

There are so many hidden meanings and messages that can be parallels to faith, religion, surrendering, suffering, temptation, and the continuous battle of good versus evil. I believe this is what made this movie so popular (along with mind-blowing special effects). The story was phenomenal and relatable.

There are many who would rather *not* hear the truth. They would rather live their lives purposefully blind and ignorant, selfishly refusing to see and hear the truth. It is much easier that way. But I believe that time is running out. There is too much at stake.

SURRENDER

The souls of every one of us need to hear the truth. I am hoping, with God's help, that I can somehow tap into the Matrix and open up some eyes and loosen the blockage to some ears so that those who are able to still be saved might hear the truth and believe. (Before it is too late!)

I look forward to seeing how God uses this material to reach the lost, open the eyes of those who may be blind, and to hopefully crack open the hardness of people's hearts so that their lives may begin to be transformed and changed for something else worth so much more than what this world has to offer.

In the beginning of this chapter, I began to discuss how the movie *The Matrix* (which came out on March 31, 1999) had impacted me significantly by effectively illuminating the unraveling of the world. The concept of the movie should provoke you to think, "Am I living in someone else's fabricated reality or am I living for the truth?"

But even more so, how much truth exists in this metaphor of choosing to take the red pill or the blue pill? The question all of us must ask is this: "If I choose to take the red pill, how deep do I really want to go down this rabbit hole?" Honestly, I believe, most people just want the blue pill and pretend there is nothing seriously bad happening and choose rather to just go on with their daily routine blindly, comfortably, and believe that our government is going to fix all our problems. They are choosing instead to believe that there is *no* rabbit hole. Hmmm, nope. Not me. I am not taking that road!

I am choosing the road less traveled.

I don't know about you, but I *really* want to go as deep as I can go. Therefore, I will be taking the red pill, or more accurately, I already *have* swallowed the red pill. Because you see, I am tired, really tired, of watching the foolishness of the hearts of men and women who seriously do not have our best interests at the forefront of doing what is best for everyone for the good of all. Our world has become a selfish foundation on almost every level. Please don't even get me started.

It is *no wonder* that Jesus came. If we *ever* needed a Savior, we need him now! The utter foolishness of man, the darkness of the hearts of people, the fruit that is so plainly seen, which is rotten fruit by the way, is simply crazy and quite honestly makes no sense. But take heart! Truly take heart and do not lose hope because Jesus has *already* overcome the world! This is our saving grace to those who believe. Millions of babies murdered will be and are already in heaven saving grace. Billions deceived by the Science, Jesus provides that saving grace. Pronouns, sexual ideologies, gender dysphoria…saving grace.

On and on we can go, down that rabbit hole to reveal so much of the pure evil that exists around every corner. But the story does not end there. Jesus has already *won the war*. Saving grace, and oh man, his amazing grace.

> Our warfare is with evil within us and around us, and we ought to be persuaded that we are able to get the victory and that we shall do so in the name of the Lord Jesus. (Charles Spurgeon)

The *most* powerful choice you can choose right now is which pill are you going to take. Who do you follow? In whom do you serve? Time is running out. You have heard this before, but many do not take this to heart. Time is running out. God will give you only so much time to *know* him. Either your heart and life are for him or you live your life in such a way to be against him. Your "fruit" will be exposed for all to see. Please make sure you are on the right side of God.

> The people who offend you with truth do not hate you. The people who comfort you with lies hate you. And if you prefer a comfortable lie over an offensive truth—you must hate yourself. (Anonymous)

The main theme of this book, I believe, which God has been showing me over the course of the last six months or so is this: to surrender.

Surrender your life to him. Surrender your will to his. Surrender your finances, your marriage, your kids, your pain, your addictions, your sadness, and your frustrations to his will. Surrender your heart, your thoughts, your sin, your faults to him. Surrender it all to him! *No one* knows better what it is that you need or even more so what you do *not* need than Jesus. If we would *only* choose to surrender our full will into his hands with absolute trust and faith, many would be blown away with what would take place in their lives.

The *transformation* is a metamorphosis beyond anything we can comprehend because it is beyond us, beyond anything we can understand. It would be like a caterpillar to a butterfly. Captivating and painful. But oh, so wonderful and necessary. Do you want to fly?

> Blessed be the God and Father of our Lord Jesus Christ! By His great mercy He has given us new birth into a living hope through the resurrection of Jesus Christ from the dead. (Peter, 1 Peter 1:3)

Please be prepared, if you decide to take the red pill, metaphorically of course, you may experience the most gratifying, exonerating, soul-wrenching, heart-expanding, eye-opening, mind-bending, tears-a-flowing, life-changing, world-banishing, Satan-attacking time of your life. This is what it means to be dangerous for Christ! When you choose to step in faith, away from the world, taking the red pill, you are doing exactly what the fish are doing in the opening monologue of my favorite show, *The Chosen*. They are swimming against the flow of the other fish. They are going against the flow of the stream. They have chosen to follow the Rabbi and not the world. They are cutting themselves off from the Matrix and experiencing the Truth, the Way, and the Life which is Jesus.

> Do not conform to the pattern of this world but be transformed by the renewing of your mind. Then you will be able to test and approve what God's will is—His good, pleasing and perfect will. (Paul, Romans 12:2)

I will be covering as many topics as I can as the Holy Spirit guides me to open doors and windows that many people want to keep shut. I will hopefully and humbly bring into the light that maybe ignorance is bliss until the time comes when there is no more time. The ignorance you once cherished will now be put before you as you will have to answer to your Creator in the choices you made, the decisions you chose in deciding that your sin in your eyes wasn't a sin or, if you ever thought, *There never was a God to begin with therefore I can do whatever I damn well please.* Judgment day will come for us all. There is no escaping death (unless you are one of the lucky ones to be raptured), and there is no escaping the day of judgment. This is not a scare tactic; this is truth.

> The Bible remains the greatest self-help book ever written because it doesn't make existence about you. It demands that you orient outside of yourself toward God. You can't help yourself if you're oriented toward yourself. You are the problem. (Ben Shapiro)

> Very truly I tell you, whoever hears my word and believes Him who sent me has eternal life and will not be judged but has crossed over from death to life. (Jesus, John 5:24)

The journey to wisdom cannot be rushed. When you eventually come to the point of finding yourself at a level of understanding to which you are then overwhelmed with awe, that is when God decides it is time for you to know just a little bit more. He will then crack open the curtain for you to taste and see the goodness of his will, not only for your life, but for the good of mankind.

This does not mean it will be easy. In fact, it will be the hardest thing you will ever do.

I have said this before, and I will say it again, this life, this world, this is not about you. When every soul comes to that truth, that piece of wisdom, then it can begin to make sense. And I mean, begin.

There has to be a beginning. There has to come a point where you proclaim, "I can't do this anymore!" There has to be that rock-bottom moment when you *surrender*: "I am done!"

Does any of this matter in the grand scheme of things? Does it matter what car you drive? Does it matter what house you live in? What career do you have? How much money do you make? Or how many vacations do you take?

Do the awards satisfy you? Do the relationships make you happy? Are you fulfilled?

I want to quote something I heard recently, and it is spot on in the world we live in and how Jesus is trying to get our attention. Trying to pull us away from that which will ultimately kill us here on earth and in the afterlife in eternity.

> Indiana Jones and the Last Crusade! Which should have been The Last Crusade. They made two more. That's a different thing. There's a moment when that cup of life falls down this crevasse and this girl, who has been kind of playing both sides, good and evil, you don't know where she's going to go, is going for the cup and she slips and is about to fall and Indy grabs her arm. And she's trying to grab this cup, the Holy Grail, that will give her fame and wealth and life. And he's saying, "Your hand is slipping, girl, I can't hold you."
>
> But in her desperate attempt to grab this, she lets go of Indy's hand, which was keeping her alive, and she plummets into the abyss. Then Indy falls into the crevasse and his dad grabs his hand and Indy starts to reach for the same cup. "But that's the cup of life, that'll give me power and influence and fame. The best artifact I could ever find, as an adventurer looking for these

things," and his dad is saying, "I'm losing a grip on you, you have to stop grabbing for the cup." And then he just says his name, "Indiana let it go." And he lets go and he grabs his father's hand, and his father saves his life.

That's what Jesus is doing here. Jesus is saying, "Hey, the way you are reaching and clutching for things that will fade, you'll fade with it." So, release transient things, and grip onto the one who will give you life. (Pastor Ben Stuart)

He is no fool who gives what he cannot keep to gain what he cannot lose. (Jim Elliott)

As I write these words, please know that I am not any greater or smarter than you. I am not wiser or more skilled, more intelligent, or more successful. I am just a broken man, like you, trying to figure it all out. But what I have learned on this journey, I am trying to share with you. We *need* each other. We need to share our struggles, our victories, our moments of loss, and our moments of being found.

I am often struggling in certain areas of my life, and that is a challenge that will probably never dissipate. The struggles will change, but the challenge is real. This is life. And sometimes, it sucks. For many, it is a constant battle day in and day out. But there is hope.

Until we realize that we are not in control but out of control is the day we realize that God *is in* control. This world may seem out of control, but be rest assured, God is most definitely in control.

Surrender. This is the moment, this is the action that must take place. But this will also be a very difficult action to fulfill. Why? Because we are selfish. We *believe* we know better than God. Ha! What a joke. But we all do it. We *choose* to not let go and let God mostly out of fear. Fearful of what will happen, what will come next, what we will have to sacrifice as we become more in tune to the Truth. More in tune to the wisdom of Christ and therefore see the world as it really is…the Matrix.

SURRENDER

Satan wants to keep you confused. Satan wants to keep you busy with your face glued to some screen device filling your mind with everything *but* God and his goodness. Temptation, sin, shame, guilt, unworthy, unwanted, not good enough, failure! Sound familiar? This is the continuous lie fed into your psyche to make you *believe* that your faults, your sin, your repeated failures of losing to temptation makes you unqualified to be a son or daughter of the King. *Beep*...wrong answer!

If you continue to fall for that trap and believe the lies, *he has you*. I know; this was me for years. Years did I struggle to believe I was loved unconditionally. For years, I believed I would never amount to anything for God to be proud of. And it wasn't until I realized and heard the words that forever changed how I saw myself through the eyes of Christ did I finally choose to allow myself to be loved.

> There is therefore now *no condemnation* for those who are in Christ Jesus. (Paul, Romans 8:1 [emphasis mine])

Bam! *This* was the beginning of my surrendering.

When you *choose* to read and digest God's Word, and this is also a form of surrender, will you then be given the opportunity to see with clarity the truth that is sitting right before your very eyes. The red pill.

Until you choose to do this and believe with faith in the one who created you and died for you, you will continue to struggle to understand or believe that you *are* worthy of God's love and that he loves you *passionately* and *completely*. You don't have to change to receive his love, but he is ready to help you change.

What I love about the Matrix is, is that in its own way, it portrayed Neo as the *one* who would bring an end to the tyranny and control that the Matrix has had on everyone. Much in the same way that Jesus does and has done and continues to do. Jesus is the hero. He is the Savior. Truth will be completely revealed, and the evil of the world will be vanquished. All those in power will have to kneel before the Lord and answer for their wicked ways. Justice will prevail. Good conquers evil.

> Do not take revenge, my dear friends, but leave room for God's wrath, for it is written: "It is mine to avenge; I will repay," says the Lord. (Paul, Romans 12:19)

The most beautiful peace comes upon us once we understand the power of surrendering our lives over to Jesus. Please don't misunderstand me, it is never easy; otherwise, there would be no cost. But to pick up your cross and follow the Rabbi also means you must surrender to his good and perfect will. Trust and obey. Have faith and believe. All these are characteristics that become a part of who you are when Jesus becomes number 1 in your life.

This life, your life, becomes *not* about you but all for him.

But in the process, you become the best part of you, you will ever be. You become like Jesus. Which is *exactly* where you want to be. You become less as he becomes more.

> A person who calls himself "Christian" and makes no effort to live the sanctified life has no right to that name. (John Calvin)

> Faith is when you stop believing what you see and begin to see what you believe. (Kathryn Kuhlman)

> Take the red pill…and let's go on this adventure…together…and then we will see how deep the rabbit hole goes.

> Since the children have flesh and blood, He too shared in their humanity so that by His death He might destroy him who holds the power of death—that is, the devil—and free those who

all their lives were held in slavery by their fear of death. For surely it is not angels He helps, but Abraham's descendants. For this reason, He had to be made like His brothers in every way, in order that He might become a merciful and faithful high priest in service to God, and that He might make atonement for the sins of the people. Because He Himself suffered when He was tempted, He is able to help those who are being tempted. (Hebrews 2:14–18)

Wherever I am, whatever I am doing, I hope and pray to God that I will have the courage to stand up for the real Jesus of the New Testament, regardless of whom I offend.

—A. W. Tozer, *A Man of God*

CHAPTER 2

Unashamed

Whoever is ashamed of me and of my words, of him will the Son of Man be ashamed when He comes in His glory and the glory of the Father and of the holy angels.
—Jesus, Luke 9:26

Whatever you are not changing…you are choosing. Read that again.
—TobyMac, #speaklife

Before I begin this chapter and before you begin to read it, I will be diving deep into this subject matter, and I want to forewarn you to take it slow. Digest what I am attempting to say. Read it slower than you normally would and let it sink in. I hope you hear this message, a message presented with love.

I don't think I have told this story before, but if I have, I apologize.

Years ago, when I was a teenager, I had this nightmare that has never left my conscience. In fact, it is a great reminder of how close I am, if I so choose, to the fall into the dark side of me.

I was sixteen, and I woke up in absolute terror as I just witnessed something in my dream that scared me into next week. I had just entered the bathroom of the apartment my mom and I rented. As I stepped in and began to close the door behind me, I did what I always did after entering the bathroom. I scanned myself in the mirror as most teenagers do. But behind the door, as it was closing, emerged an evil exact copy of myself as I shrunk with absolute horror. With much distress, I looked at the image of myself as it was looking back at me, and my spine shrieked and my body was covered in goosebumps as the terror in my eyes of the evil me gave me such an evil look with a wicked, crooked smile and a demonized trance that I froze with a loss of breath and then woke with my heart pounding and in absolute shock.

It was intensely frightening. Just like straight out of a horror flick. And I have never forgotten the feeling I had that moment when I awoke from that nightmare. It was almost as if I needed to see this side of me, the possibility of me becoming a formulation of the dark side. To lose oneself into this world, believing that this world has something more to offer. There are many, many who choose to walk the dark path. Sadly, they believe in the darkness and the ruler who lives there, choosing to serve the darkness instead of the light yet deny the Creator who created them. This baffles me to no end! Why would someone literally choose to be in a place of never-ending darkness? The answer is quite simple: power, greed, addictions, sex… the list goes on. They get to choose who is in control and who has the power. Those who live for the dark side believe they have the power and everything that Jesus stands for goes against their theology, their ideology, their darkness. It goes against everything this world deems good and right. Their will becomes far more important than God's will for their lives.

> Decisions become easier when your will to please God outweighs your will to please the world. (TobyMac, #speaklove)

But here is the kicker: there are many who proclaim to be Christian, followers of Christ, Christlike, who still do the same things as those who worship the devil. They choose to be "of the world" instead of being "not of this world." So which is it? Are you ashamed of Christ? Are you ashamed to act like Christ, proclaim Christ as your Lord and Savior, turn away from the world and the sin that is so prevalent in your life? Do you go to church on Sunday and then live how you want on Monday? Does your life have any representation of Jesus? Any fruit?

> Too many of us...want a seat...at tables that Jesus would've flipped over. (TobyMac, #speaklove)

Read that sentence again.
Until you *see* and *believe* the truth, choose to live out this truth, admit your sins, truly and genuinely ask for forgiveness, seek out Jesus with your whole heart, whole life, surrendering to his will. You will continue down this path of unrighteousness, ashamed of the gospel and ashamed to share, and show with action, to explain to others of your relationship with Jesus. To truly repent of your sins is to stand tall and acknowledge them aloud. Do it! Make a list of the sins you know you have committed; ask Jesus for forgiveness. *Accept his forgiveness*! You can even identify two or three believers you trust to accept your repentance with *grace* and share your sins with them so the enemy can no longer hold them over your head. He cannot make you feel shame for something you have released. He cannot control you if *you* don't let him!

Consider this, I have discussed the verses I am going to share with you now before in my other books, and it is more frightening than the nightmare I shared with you earlier.

> I never knew you! (Jesus, Matthew 7:23)

I want you to imagine for just a moment. In fact, close your eyes for a moment and imagine yourself standing in front of Jesus on the day of judgment. He is about to open the book on your life and reveal all that you have done while on earth. He will proclaim with absolute clarity the dark and ugly stains of sin that has been put there by you if, of course, you have chosen to live for the selfishness of the world, the materialistic world, full of sin, sex, debauchery, lies, stealing, greed, murder, envy, etc. And all you have to proclaim, all you have to offer, is your perfect attendance at church every Sunday; you even told someone you would pray for them, but never did. You have a plethora of knowledge of the scriptures, but you have chosen *not* to apply them to your life.

You struggle with pornography, or maybe you just struggle a little bit, getting a peek here and there through R-rated movies or in magazines, playing it off like it is normal. Or your life is moving in the right direction: you're financially stable, your kids are healthy, and your marriage is pretty good. You feel strong, secure, and successful; your career is on fire, and life is good.

You've got a Tesla in the garage, a 3,000-square-foot house with four bedrooms and two full baths. Golfing twice a month, part of the Rotary, and plenty of friends. Oh, and you also sponsor two kids in Cambodia.

Now imagine for a moment that you just had a heart attack; death came a lot earlier than expected, and now you're in darkness, separated from God, screaming with no one to hear you with weeping and gnashing of teeth in utter darkness, and you ask yourself, "How can this be? I prayed, I went to church, I knew the gospel good enough…what did I do wrong?"

> There are two types of Christians. Those who believe in God, and those who sincerely believe they believe. (Girolamo Savonarola, martyred Italian Dominican friar, story told by Richard Wurmbrand)

> On that day many will say to me, "Lord, Lord, did we not prophesy in your name, and cast out demons in your name, and do many mighty works in your name?" And then I will declare to them, "I never knew you; depart from me, you workers of lawlessness." (Jesus, Matthew 7:21–23)

Whoa…say what?

SURRENDER

This right here, those verses are the stuff nightmares are made of. If you are a believer and are right with God, this *still* should make you fear God. And that, I believe, is the point. Those who believe that they are above the law will face the law, and that face is Jesus.

This is the foundation of my existence: to *live out this life in the righteousness of* God. To be sinless in his sight, to be found righteous in doing good works and living out my life in faith and in fear and trembling. We must fear God so that the fear truthfully steers our souls in the right direction so that we may become like him in every way.

When we live out our life in our will and not that of Jesus, we are choosing to become god, and that is not what God wants for us. He has given us this warning with many others to read and follow. But many will choose a different path. I don't ever again want to live my life ashamed of who I am. Ashamed of the God I want to live for, sacrifice for, and surrender to. I choose to share with others the love that he has shown me so deeply and passionately. I am unashamed of my love for Jesus. Unashamed to shout from the mountaintops that he is my Lord and Savior, and in him do I trust!

> So do not be ashamed to testify about our Lord, or ashamed of me His prisoner. But join with me in suffering for the Gospel, by the power of God, who has saved us and called us to a holy life—not because of anything we have done but because of His own purpose and grace. This grace was given us in Christ Jesus before the beginning of time, but it has now been revealed through the appearing of our Savior, Christ Jesus, who has destroyed death and has brought life and immortality to light through the Gospel. (Paul, 2 Timothy 1:8–11)

The guilt and the shame of our poor choices is enough to swallow us whole into an abyss of never-ending abuse, not only in our minds and hearts of whom we have allowed ourselves to be, but also into the understanding of how we feel God might look upon us and in the failure we believe we have become. We are deeply ashamed of those whom we have hurt so we feel unworthy, unacceptable, not wanted and cast aside. Which in turn gives us the feeling of being unloved and not cared for.

But I have a secret: it is never over as long as you have breath in your lungs and a pulse in your veins. Amazing grace is exactly that—amazing. You *can* turn this ship around. You can begin anew. You can, again, be forgiven because his grace and mercy never end. But *you* must want it. *You* have to genuinely want to be different. *You* must find a way to walk away and leave the world behind before God leaves you behind (rapture). And *nobody* wants that. Nobody. Except those who have chosen to serve themselves and not sell out to God.

> What makes authentic disciples is not visions, ecstasies, biblical mastery of chapter and verse, or spectacular success in the ministry, but a capacity for faithfulness. Buffeted by the fickle winds of failure, battered by their own unruly emotions, and bruised by rejection and ridicule, authentic disciples may have stumbled and frequently fallen, endured lapses and relapses, gotten handcuffed to the fleshpots and wandered into a far country. Yet, they kept coming back to Jesus. (Brennan Manning)

This description you just read of authentic disciples is a perfect depiction of me. Absolutely *me*!

I am that broken mess, but Jesus. I am that failure, but Jesus.

I am filled with unruly emotions and too much zealousness, but Jesus. I have been ridiculed and rejected many, many times, but Jesus.

I have stumbled and fallen more times than days I have lived, but Jesus.

I have relapsed into the world of flesh, fantasy, lust, and desire beyond all that I care to repeat, but Jesus.

SURRENDER

I have wept uncontrollably in the arms of Jesus in his loving arms, forgiven again and again. And it was Jesus who *never* gave up on me. It was me who gave up on me. It was me who was ashamed. And it was Jesus who kept showing me that he has something better than what this world had to offer.

And then, I finally listened. I *finally* had the courage to give up the world and completely surrender my life to him.

> Do your best to present yourself to God as one approved, a workman who does not need to be ashamed and who correctly handles the word of truth. (Paul, 2 Timothy 2:15)

Until we come to that point, the point of *only* wanting to live for Jesus, we will live in some level of shame. Because in all honesty and truthfulness, we are still only serving ourselves unless we are *all in for* Jesus.

> Well done good and faithful servant! Come and share in your Master's happiness. (Jesus, Matthew 25:23)

> Do nothing out of selfish ambition or vain conceit. Rather, in humility value others above yourselves, not looking to your own interests but each of you to the interests of others. (Paul, Philippians 2:3–4)

There are many to whom believe that our social status, our job titles, accolades, trophies, plaques, salaries, awards, rewards, company cars, and wealth paint the picture of our success, our identity, and who we are and what we have become without blinking an eye as to what these mean in the greater scheme of things.

One of my favorite things to read are the stories and parables that Jesus tells the crowds in an attempt to crack open their hardened hearts to the truth. Or to the point of attempting to crack through the surface of their elephant-skin exterior in hopes of reaching the interior of the heart and soul of mankind.

This parable is a perfect example of this. And what is interesting about this parable is that this is the only parable in which Jesus gave a name to someone within it. This is the rich man and the beggar.

> There was a rich man who was dressed in purple and fine linen and lived in luxury every day. At his gate was laid a beggar named Lazarus, covered with sores and longing to eat what fell from the rich man's table. Even the dogs came and licked his sores.
>
> The time came when the beggar died and the angels carried him to Abraham's side. The rich man also died and was buried. In hell, where he was in torment, he looked up and saw Abraham far away, with Lazarus by his side. So he called to him, "Father Abraham, have pity on me and send Lazarus to dip the tip of his finger in water to cool my tongue, because I am in agony in this fire."
>
> But Abraham replied, "Son, remember that in your lifetime you received your good things, while Lazarus received bad things, but now he is comforted here and you are in agony. And besides all this, between us and you a great chasm has been fixed, so that those who want to go from here to you cannot, nor can anyone cross over from there to us."
>
> He answered, "Then I beg you, father, send Lazarus to my father's house, for I have five brothers. Let him warn them, so that they will not also come to this place of torment."
>
> Abraham replied, "They have Moses and the Prophets; let them listen to them."
>
> "No father Abraham," he said, "but if someone from the dead goes to them, they will repent."

SURRENDER

> He said to him, "If they do not listen to Moses and the Prophets, they will not be convinced even if someone rises from the dead." (Jesus, Luke 16:19–31)

This is a powerful parable in quite a few different ways. And there are challenging lessons to be learned through this story. How many of us want to skip over the reality that is so blatantly obvious in the fact that a rich man, which many of us are compared to the rest of the world, don't want to attach this form of title to ourselves. We don't want to be held accountable to the fact that *we*, you and I, very fluently fit this scenario. How many times have you walked by a beggar and ignored them? How many times have you walked by a person who was in need and pretended like they weren't even there? Like they didn't even deserve your acknowledgement? They didn't deserve your measly $2? Or the extra food you had sitting next to you? I have sadly. And I regret that I have done so.

Now, please understand, there are many of you reading this who have given generously or at least gave what you had and that is commendable. But in the grand scheme of things and to be completely honest and forthright with ourselves, how much—within all that has been given to you by God because all of this all the money, houses, land, cars, by the way, are not yours, they are God's—how much have we truly given to those who are in need? How much of what God has given us have we given away?

Be honest with yourself and take a moment to *really* think about that. Go ahead. I will wait.

Now, take this all into consideration because I believe we must. It is healthy and wise to be conscientious of how we view the commands and warnings of Christ. We need to be completely honest with ourselves to those who truly follow Christ, to heed his words, to heed his warnings. These should be at the top of our list of things we should be taking inventory of in our everyday lives.

Even now, this very moment, I have been challenged by God in listening to the Holy Spirit's conviction on me that I have too much stuff. I heard, through prayer, a few days ago, "Would you be willing to give it all away for me and my kingdom? Give it away and give the money to the poor?" Which I replied through tears, "Yes, Lord, I would." And so, begins the process of elimination. It is time to donate my belongings, my collectibles, because let's be real, they are just sitting on shelves or in glass cases collecting dust and for what? To display for all to see? I know that what I have is not mine, but it is God's. But it is up to me to decide what I will do with what he has given me. I would rather have treasures in heaven than treasures on earth.

Our very existence is based on becoming the hands and feet of Christ, his soldiers, his voice. The scriptures, time and time again, make it very clear what and where our true focus lies. But if we are simply unaware of what those scriptures say because we are not *reading* them, then we may not know how we are supposed to be doers of the Word. This is where you might want to check yourself before you wreck yourself.

One of the most used phrases or excusable phrases that have been applied to the Christian faith is that we are saved by grace and not by works. Which is completely true. We are most definitely saved by the blood of Christ and his sacrifice on the cross, not because of something we either need to do or choose to do. That falls more along the lines of religion. Following Christ is not checking off boxes with a check mark as you move down the Christian to-do list so that at the end of the day, you feel like you earned your salvation. You cannot earn your salvation, it is a free gift.

The *change* comes with growth in your walk with Jesus as you grow closer in your relationship with him. As you read and learn and become more aware of how Jesus lived, what Jesus said, and digging into the New Testament, you begin to understand how to live out your life Christlike. That is the whole point: we are attempting to become like Jesus. Not become a god. That is impossible. But to truly live out our lives seeking after the heart of Christ.

> Therefore, I urge you, brothers, in view of God's mercy, to offer your bodies as living sacrifices, holy and pleasing to God—this is your

> spiritual act of worship. Do not conform any longer to the pattern of this world, but be transformed by the renewing of your mind. Then you will be able to test and approve what God's will is—His good, pleasing and perfect will. (Paul, Romans 12:1–2)

I remember when I was in high school, I had a really difficult time trying to live out my life as an example of my faith. I was torn. And it was painful. Hormones, girls, peer pressure…the whole gamut. I was a wreck because of my toxic home life and a wreck because of how difficult it truly was to try and fit into my life any chance of living out and acting out my life as someone who follows and believes in Jesus. Needless to say, I failed miserably. In fact, it took me until I was in my thirties to finally feel like I was on to something and living out my faith without any reservations. I became less and less unashamed of my faith and began to share it with anyone who asked or was curious why I was the way I was.

If we consider Bible verses, such as the ones that mention and clarify that we are saved by the grace of Jesus and not by works, but then use that as a scapegoat to choose to not move in the direction of living out your life like Christ in being a doer of the Word, you are missing a huge chunk of truly living out an unashamed life for Christ. And that would not stand up in a case before Jesus. He *wants* to see change. He *wants* to see growth. He *wants* to see action which is wrapped up beautifully and deeply in the Great Commandment. He wants a relationship with you. And no relationship succeeds if it is one-sided. You have to be committed. You have to be devoted.

> G: Get on your knees and pray.
> R: Read your Bible daily.
> O: Offer your body as a living sacrifice.
> W: Worship in Spirit and in Truth.

"Teacher, which is the greatest commandment in the law?" Jesus replied: "Love the Lord your God with all your heart and with all your soul and with all your mind. This is the first and greatest commandment. And the second is like it: Love your neighbor as yourself." (Jesus, Matthew 22:36–39)

If we dissect these verses, Jesus is saying that to love God, we must do what?

Love him with *all* your heart, *all* your soul, *all* your mind, and love everyone, every neighbor, *as you love yourself.* Does this simply mean that I will love everyone and God if and when I come into contact with people and I show them love and respect while opening the door for them, saying excuse me, bless them when they sneeze, compliment them, sponsor a few kids around the world, pray for people, read my daily devotional, go to and participate in Bible study, and make it to church every Sunday? Well, yes. But does it end there? I don't think so. Let's read a few more verses just to clarify what is being expected of us.

In the fifth chapter of Matthew, after Jesus presents the Beatitudes, he says this: "Blessed are you when people insult you, persecute you and falsely say all kinds of evil against you because of me. Rejoice and be glad, because great is your reward in heaven, for in the same way they persecuted the prophets who were before you" (Jesus, Matthew 5:11–12).

So why would Jesus say something like this to those who would become followers of him? I don't believe it too difficult to figure out that to be in a position where you are having insults thrown at you or that you are being persecuted or have people saying all sorts of evil against you; it won't happen when we are being kind to someone. It won't happen when we are opening a door for someone or any other kind gesture. It will be because you are living out your life in such a way that those who are having offense against you are doing so simply because they see by your words and by your actions that you love Jesus and are not afraid to proclaim it or to be doing something that is an example of loving others with the love of Jesus. You are acting out as Christ would, and you are *not* ashamed.

SURRENDER

And rightly so.

Then, in the next four verses, Jesus says this:

> You are the salt of the earth. But if the salt loses its saltiness, how can it be made salty again? It is no longer good for anything, except to be thrown out and trampled by men. You are the light of the world. A city on a hill cannot be hidden. Neither do people light a lamp and put it under a bowl. Instead, they put it on a stand, and it gives light to everyone in the house. In the same way, let your light shine before men, that they may see your good deeds and praise your Father in heaven. (Jesus, Matthew 5:13–16)

If a seasoning has no flavor, it has no value. This is exactly what Jesus is saying here in verses 13–16: if you are not salty, you have no value. If you are hiding your light, your faith, your love for Jesus, your Christlikeness, then you are showing by your lack of action that you are ashamed of Jesus. If you are only believing that being a Christian is about accepting Christ into your heart, saying the prayer and then choosing to not live out your faith in Jesus and, in turn, *not* shine your light before men, then there is a good chance that Jesus may say to you one day, "I never knew you."

Trust me, you don't *ever* want to hear that.

> Whoever acknowledges me before men, I will also acknowledge him before my Father in heaven. But whoever disowns me before men, I will disown him before my Father in heaven. (Jesus, Matthew 10:32–33)

Yes, we are saved by grace, not by works, but I do believe *very* strongly that Jesus has made it very clear throughout scripture, and I could give you twenty more verses that fall in line with these verses I have just quoted, which would suggest that he has expectations of us as believers to pick up our cross daily, deny ourselves, meaning to die to one's self and follow him wholeheartedly.

Unashamed!

This is just the beginning of many subjects that God wants me to share with you. To prayerfully and hopefully shine light on the depth of Jesus, his words, parables, commandments, his truth, his way, his life so that we can become more like him in every way. But even more importantly, with action, with compassion, with patience and an understanding that this is part of the journey.

Jesus lived out his life dangerously. Many people wanted to kill him, even his own people from his own hometown. Why? Because they were offended by his words, proclaiming that he was the Christ, the Messiah that they had been waiting for. It didn't matter that he did miracles. It didn't matter that his wisdom, his wealth of knowledge of the scriptures, and his storytelling were off the charts. They wanted to kill him because they simply did not believe that he could be the One they had been waiting for all those hundreds of years. And he went against their religion, their rules, and challenged them, very wisely I must say, and with strong scriptural doctrine, to their ways and beliefs of the Law that was given to them. which they used very legalistically. And Jesus did not like this at all. They wanted to kill him simply because he stood up and told them, they (the Pharisees, Sadducees, and the Sanhedrin) were wrong, and he was going to prove it.

> Many people reject Jesus because of bad experiences with religious people. But, here's the thing...Jesus had bad experiences with religious people, too. In fact, they killed him. People will let you down. Jesus won't. (Anonymous)

When you choose to follow Christ, it is not, or should not be, taken lightly. Jesus says, "Count the cost." There is honestly very little to no wiggle room to be a follower of Jesus. Simply because we are *choosing* to "Not be of this world." We are choosing to go against the mainstream of all that the world views as important or views as solid truth, the "right way" or the "moral" way. "Trust the science" is one of many social sayings that have become a "believe it or be ridiculed" kind of fashion from around the world.

It has become taboo to challenge anything that is not supported by the mainstream media and especially if you try and match the world's views to that of scripture, you are instantly made out to be a bigot, a racist, a heretic, a hypocrite, or some other politically driven name-calling that falls in line with what I quoted above from Matthew. "Blessed are you when people insult you, persecute you, and falsely say all kinds of evil against you because of me" (Jesus, Matthew 5:11).

This has become the absolute norm throughout the whole world. What once was known to be wrong is now right. And that which has known to be right since the beginning of time is now considered wrong (or at least, unpopular). Sadly, it has also become welcomed even among the church. There are, of course, many different denominations or belief systems within churches who teach a watered-down doctrine of the Bible or they teach only parts of the Bible that fit into their ideology or man-made theology that is between them and God. But when we deny the scriptures and decide that we know better than God and choose to follow suit into the ways of the world, that is dangerous ground, shaky ground, a house built on sand.

Please know and truly understand that there are many, many people who are hurting and who feel unloved or that God has abandoned them. I get it. And I would never want to miss out on an opportunity to show them that they are loved; every walk of life matters. God loves them all and so should we.

Does this mean we must fall into place and obey the world's commands that just because this person or that person decided that they are a long-haired female cat and that we must now follow suit and treat this person, who was born a human male, as a female feline? I don't think so. That is absolute foolishness. I will respect their decision. Respect them as the human they are, but this does not mean I have to obey and follow and be a part of the circus. Give me a flippin' break.

> In a world full of people who prefer to be called by pronouns, I've decided that I want to

be known by adjectives. A few examples would be…Saved, redeemed, delivered, rescued, forgiven, justified, born-again, and sanctified. (Anonymous)

> A new command I give you: Love one another. As I have loved you, so you must love one another…So, I am giving you a new command: Love each other. (Jesus, John 13:34)

I have found that on this journey of mine, to love one another is truly the most profound way that we can show who we are and who we call Lord. People are tired of words without action. People are watching to see if someone who proclaims that they are followers of the Rabbi that their life reflects that. That their actions reflect that. That their love mirrors exactly what they proclaim. Too many people who used words and then failed to back that up have failed those who wanted to see with action that they lived out their faith, that they walked the walk, not just talked the talk.

Live out your life with fear and trembling of a God who loves you, yes, but never forget that he can also deny he ever knew you simply because you chose the world instead of him.

It *all matters*. Be a doer of the Word, and live your life out loud; live unashamed of your love for Jesus. Make him known and show the world through your love and through your actions that Jesus is alive and well in your heart, in your soul, and in your mind while loving your neighbor *as yourself.*

> Every tree that does not bear good fruit is cut down and thrown into the fire. Therefore, by their fruits you will know them. (Jesus, Matthew 7:19–20)

> You will not find on this side of heaven a holier people than those who receive into their

SURRENDER

hearts the doctrine of Christ's righteousness. (Charles Spurgeon)

Consider this quote from Rev. Billy Graham:

> They first took off His clothes…then they took long leather thongs with steel pellets or lead pellets on the end and beat Him across the back and legs until He could barely stand up. Then they put a crown of thorns on his brow and His face was bleeding. And they laughed at Him, and they spit on Him, and they mocked Him. And with one snap of His fingers…72,000 angels had already drawn their swords ready to come to His rescue and wipe this planet out of existence in the universe.
>
> And Jesus said, "No. To this end was I born."
>
> He wasn't just another revolutionary. He wasn't just another hippie. He was not just another great man. He was God in the flesh. And all the ethics that He taught…never a man spoke like that man. When you get hit on one side, He says to turn the other cheek. He never said what to do after that. But He did say forgive 70 times 7…count that out. Jesus taught that we were to forgive…He taught a revolution in the way we are to live. He taught us that it wasn't just our outward actions that God judges but it's the inward thoughts that He counts. And He dragged and He lifted and hauled that cross. He didn't squirm…He didn't yell…He didn't scream. He just took it…and said, *"Lord forgive them… they don't know what they are doing."*
>
> When He died on that cross…they nailed Him…they put the nails in His hands. And you

know what He said..."*Forgive them...they know not what they do.*" Forgive them...could you forgive someone that's putting nails in your hands and you know you didn't deserve it? Then look at the death He died. Did ever a man die like Jesus? The lightning flashed and the thunder roared, and the earth began to shake... and *even* the soldiers confessed that this must be the Son of God!

Anyone who can see Jesus on that cross and not be touched has a heart of stone. And then... *on the cross*...He said, *"My God, my God, why has thou forsaken me?"* And then He dropped His head and said... *"It is finished!"*

What did He mean? He meant God's plan of salvation was finished. God can now forgive you of all your sins because Jesus had finished God's plan for your salvation. (Billy Graham)

But He was pierced for our transgressions. He was crushed for our iniquities: The punishment that brought us peace was on Him, and by His wounds we are healed. (Isaiah 53:5)

If being hurt by the church causes you to lose faith in God, then your faith was in people…*not God*!

CHAPTER 3

Crashing through Existence

God is not going to rewrite the Bible for your generation. Stop trying to change Scripture when it's written to change you.
—Anonymous

Do nothing out of selfish ambition or vain conceit.
Rather, in humility value others above yourselves.
—Paul, Philippians 2:3

Frodo: I wish none of this had happened.
Gandalf: So do all who live to see such times, but that is not for them to decide. All we have to decide is what to do with the time that is given to us. There are other forces at work in this world, Frodo, besides the will of evil. Bilbo was meant to find the ring. In which case, you also were meant to have it and that is an encouraging thought.
—J. R. R. Tolkien, *The Lord of the Rings*

Each and every generation believes that its problems, its challenges, and the dysfunctions that come with it is something new to this world, and they decide to say it loud and proud. Generally speaking, this is true. But in the vast expanse of history and all that comes with it, there is a reverberating noise that continues to bounce off the walls of insecurity. And with it, a familiar sickening odor that

SURRENDER

continues to stick to the very souls of so many who fall for this trap. Lies of the devil are wickedly profound. He is a thief who is looking to steal your soul all the while feeding into your philosophy or your ideology or your greed and sexual desires and what you believe to be your identity, and with it, everything you want to hear that gives you some form of purpose or a place to belong where you feel you are welcomed. Basically, he is distracting you from God and distorting your reality.

We are all so easily enticed. Cupping our ears with our hands seeking out desperately to find the noise that soothes and pacifies us.

Life has a way of bending us like clay so we can fit into the box that has been made for us in a world that pretends it has our best interests at heart. The trickiest part of this life within the many boxes lying before us is really to take a moment or as long as it takes really to notice and evaluate if this box or that box is truly where we fit in or even belong. Who made this box? Who made this clay? Who am I? Or even better, where did this glass jar come from?

If we stop for just a moment, and hopefully more than just a moment, to take in all that is around us and not just what is right in front of us, it is possible that we may begin to see a much bigger picture. Like instead of only seeing boxes, we start to see glass jars. Instead of only seeing anger, murder, death, wars, we can start to see life, miracles, beauty, love, grace, and forgiveness.

It may seem, and is probably true, that I am speaking in riddles, but I do have a point I am trying to make here.

Instead of believing what is being repeatedly said as truth, may we take a moment and say, "What if what the world is saying is false? What if it is all a huge ploy and plumb full of lies, greed, and deceit? What if the science is financially motivated?" Let's take the activist position of Black Lives Matter and acknowledge it has a substantial amount of money—millions of dollars, in fact. Funds were donated to the cause and intended for a beneficial purpose but is instead only benefiting those in whom pushed this ideology and are now sitting in million-dollar homes? What if that which is being so profoundly indoctrinated and shoved into every situation and belief system, as the LGBTQ+ community is trying to do, is that this new uprising of sexual dysphoria is the new normal and the only thing that is true, and there is no other truth? Could these ideologies, communities, and so-called programs for justice might possibly have a selfish motivation and financial agenda hidden within? Is it not perhaps a little narrow-minded?

A Ben Shapiro debate over gender ideology that I found sums up clearly what most of us are thinking. Read this transcript I wrote down word for word from this debate. It is spot on!

> Pro-trans woman: I am very glad none of these opinions are actually accepted in Academia and haven't been for over 70 years.
>
> Ben Shapiro: Okay, so the notion that they haven't been accepted for over 70 years is a bizarre one...considering they were until about five minutes ago. And the basic idea that male and female do not exist runs counter to all mammalian biology. All of it, not just human. Are we to suggest that gender and sex are different in walruses? How does this work exactly? Like are they different in bears?
>
> Anytime you have all mammalian reproduction that is rooted in the idea that there's a sexual dichotomy between male and female, to obscure that with all sorts of semantic word games about how you feel subjectively...has no bearing on whether male and female are categories that exist. And if you are trying to define male and female with references to any subjective category that cannot be identified by any metric whatsoever other than how you feel today, I challenge whether that is scientific or whether that is merely a self-perception that is being guided by a political agenda.
>
> Bam!

> The simple step of a courageous individual is not to take part in the lie. (Aleksandr Solzhenitsyn)

And yes, we can take any narrative and apply it to this kind of questioning, as we should. But it sure seems that what is being shoved so deep down our throats is not an option to be considered, it is all becoming law with no chance of discussion. Sexual orientation dysphoria, pronouns, child trafficking, gender dysphoria, transgender—all of this is sweeping over our world like a tsunami wave.

Even worse yet is the sexual exploitation and trafficking of children which has now become one of the most, if not the most, lucrative financial underground marketing systems in the world. Billions upon billions of dollars are now spent on this destructive and evil empire for mere men, and a few women, to satisfy a hunger that cannot be filled by preying on children.

Have you ever stopped to ask, "How did this become such a wicked and evil thing? How did this grow to be so out of control and become such a wicked disease in so many lives of men and women throughout our world?"

I have only one answer: the sin of the flesh, lust, sex, immorality, greed, can only be satisfied by one thing, the next thing. When pornography became available to everyone through the internet, it became a disease that would spread like wildfire, and now that wildfire is out of control. Nothing will stop it. The only thing that will is the second coming of Jesus Christ.

It has recently become the norm to add the rainbow flag to school flagpoles while discriminating against any and all forms of Christianity. Or hanging rainbow flags in our school classrooms while discriminating against prayer before football games.

What this world deems as right and good goes against all that the Bible teaches and what Jesus came to earth to proclaim and help shine light upon. And they killed him for it.

There is a spiritual battle going on which is so demonic and blatantly obvious that it doesn't even seem possible. But it is, and it is happening in broad daylight.

How can we say it is okay to bring children to gay parades when there are men parading around naked with their junk hanging out for all to see? How is it okay for trans men and trans women reading to children in public schools or anywhere for that matter, stories of children, made up of course, who are struggling with their sexual identity at four, five, or six years old? How is this and so many more stories and truths of the chaos that is happening all over the world *okay* in the eyes of so many people? It's *not okay*! *It is absolutely disgusting and evil*! Plain and simple. How can this be accepted as the norm?

But this is *exactly* what is happening and even worse than this. I don't even want to know how perverse it truly gets or how dark and evil it is going to become.

But I guarantee you this, God is still in control, and all of this, *all of this evil*, all of this chaos, is happening for a reason.

If you have ever wondered why God destroyed the inhabitants of the earth before, look around. This is why. The innocence of so many beautiful babies is being destroyed with such a force that it is hard to imagine. The amount of pain and suffering in our world today because of this absolute horror of ideologies and belief systems that men can be women and women, men. That men can get pregnant. That children no longer need consent from parents to physically change their bodies, mutilate their bodies because they now believe they are no longer a girl but a boy or vice versa, and now the government will intervene and allow this to happen without a say in what the parents think? Really? This *is law*? And all of this is sane? All of this is okay? Hmmm…I don't think so.

> If a man wants to pretend he's a woman,
> that's up to him. But if he wants *us* to pretend
> he's a woman…that's up to us. (Anonymous)

You do not need to go very far or search very deep to find the atrocities happening all over the world. The confusion, the absolute meltdown of common sense is being obliterated with lies. Deceit. Conniving people push their twisted ideologies to fit their own selfish and sickening desires and that is purely to exploit children into the devilish sexual activities these people, and many in our government, want to make legal. And have already begun pushing this envelope into the hands of spineless leaders who succumb to anything that brings them more money and more power. Disgusting to the greatest degree. Inhumane and unjustly plunging these innocent children into the darkest parts of our world without any recourse or hope that something will stop it from happening.

As I, and all of you, sit back and watch one travesty after another take place, one more child goes missing, one more child is sexually abused and exploited, one more child no longer believes there is a God, I have only one hope, and that is in the name of Jesus.

> If the Bible calls it a sin...our opinion doesn't matter. (Anonymous)

He is our *only hope*. I can only find solitude and be at peace in him because I know and I believe that *all of this*, all of this is happening because we are getting *that* much closer to the end. Oh, Lord, please come back soon.

As I am writing this, Israel just declared war on Palestine, and there was another earthquake that killed thousands of people. Yes, war has been going on since the beginning of time, and yes, earthquakes too, but I am keeping watch, as are all of you. As we should and as we have been told by Jesus to do. *"Keep watch"* is what he said. And so, I do.

> It's like in the great stories, Mr. Frodo. The ones that really mattered. Full of darkness they were. And sometimes you didn't want to know the end. Because how could the end be happy? How could the world go back to the way it was when so much bad had happened?
> But in the end, it's only a passing thing, this shadow. Even darkness must pass. A new day will come. And when the sun shines...it will shine out the clearer. Those were the stories that

> stayed with you. That meant something, even if you were too small to understand why.
>
> But I think, Mr. Frodo, I do understand. I know now. Folk in those stories had lots of chances of turning back, only they didn't. They kept going, because they were holding on to something.
>
> That there is some good in this world, and it's worth fighting for. (Samwise Gamgee, *The Lord of the Rings* by J. R. R. Tolkien)

There *is* some good in this world. There is *a lot* of good in this world, but we must keep fighting for what is right, what is innocent, what is good and holy. We must stand, while we can, for the injustices of the world. Be the voice of those who have no voice, not sit on our hands and believe it will go away. Pray like never before; give generously to those who are the soldiers in the battlefield fighting to make a difference in the world. Be the light and salt in a world of so much darkness. Do not be ashamed of what you believe or what you stand for if it is for the good of the children and biblically sound.

But many have been persuaded to believe otherwise. So be it. I stand with the cross of Christ, and in him, only him, do I trust.

When we let the lies tickle our ears and then we find ourselves dancing to a different beat all the while following the pied piper on the road to hell simply because we didn't want to hurt any feelings, then we have done them, and many, an injustice. We have missed the chance to show them pure love and acceptance into the arms of Jesus.

> "Love must be sincere. Hate what is evil; cling to what is good. Be devoted to one another in brotherly love. Honor one another above yourselves. Never be lacking in zeal, but keep your spiritual fervor, serving the Lord. Be joyful in hope, patient in affliction, faithful in prayer. Share with God's people who are in need. Practice hospitality.

> "Bless those who persecute you; bless and do not curse. Rejoice with those who rejoice; mourn with those who mourn. Live in harmony with one another. Do not be proud, but be willing to associate with people of low position. Do not be conceited.
>
> "Do not repay anyone evil for evil. Be careful to do what is right in the eyes of everybody. If it is possible, as far as it depends on you, live at peace with everyone. Do not take revenge, my friends, but leave room for God's wrath, for it is written: 'It is mine to avenge; I will repay,'" says the Lord.
>
> "On the contrary: 'If your enemy is hungry, feed him; if he is thirsty, give him something to drink. In doing this, you will heap burning coals on his head.'
>
> "Do not be overcome by evil, but overcome evil with good." (Paul, Romans 12:9–21)

God's Word is so powerful in the sense that it immediately extinguishes the fire of the evil one simply done with love.

I have a good friend from high school who is a staunch atheist. Over the years, he has battled against me, viciously I might add, with his rhetoric atheistic beliefs standing up against my beliefs with many different subject titles such as abortion, evolution versus creation, the Bible and its authenticity, COVID, masks, etcetera, etcetera.

I have been as calm and as constructive as I can be in those debates that were, at times, savage verbal abuse. I never wanted this to be something that would end our friendship just because we believed differently. Although I had to end some friendships that became too toxic and came to the realization that there just wasn't anything left to salvage. It is okay to walk away from what becomes unhealthy in your life or when it becomes hurtful and damaging to you personally.

I, of course, if you haven't figured it out yet, am very passionate about my relationship with Jesus. What did it say in the verses in Romans that I just wrote a few paragraphs back?

"Never be lacking in zeal, but keep your spiritual fervor, serving the Lord."

Yep, that's me. I need to keep my zeal in check, or it ends up coming out like a flood which does no one any good.

Anyway, this good friend of mine, we have been staying in touch and remaining friends even through the differences of belief. I may never change his mind, as he will never change mine, but what my wife and I have chosen to do, because she is also good friends with him, is to love him where he is at, despite our differences. I only want to shine light and love into his life. And not necessarily with words or debate, but in true friendship and through the example of my life as a believer in Jesus. I show my obedience to Christ in my actions, not just my words.

He recently lost his father and, then a couple months later, lost his brother. They passed away suddenly, and it was devastating. The circumstances with his brother were difficult, and his father passed away from complications of old age. My wife and I knew he needed us. Not just us, but anyone who would offer love and support in any way we could. This speaks louder than words. And these opportunities are where we get to love like Jesus into their lives for no other reason or motive but to simply love them where they are at.

> When you have nothing left but God, when you have stripped yourself of everything except God, when you have taken hold of the altar and persisted in prayer, your prayers will make a difference. (Dr. Michael Youssef)

Darkness, death, evil, and sin have always been present within the very fabric of every human being who ever existed excusing only one, Jesus. He died, but he defeated death on the cross with the greatest sacrifice so we can have eternal life, if we so choose to believe. He rose again and is sitting at the right hand of the Father acting as our

Redeemer who has cleansed us of all unrighteousness. But only if we believe and follow after him.

It is inevitable and unavoidable to the end of which we all will come to see.

I have a sign at our nonprofit thrift store that reads: "Don't take life so seriously, none of us get out of here alive anyway." This brings a few chuckles to people who read this, but then the reality kicks in and then they begin to see the truth within the sarcasm.

We hear of death spoken of so often now in the news from all over the world that it has become numb to my ears and to the reality of it all, which is crazy to stop and think about. One thousand here, nine hundred there…war, a plane crash, a mass shooting, an earthquake, a flood, a raging fire…Lord, have mercy.

It becomes difficult to see clearly what lies before us as a human race. What does the rest of the story look like? None of us knows for sure. But I have a strong faith in the belief of what the Bible says about times such as these. All I can say is, you better hold on tight. We could be in for some even crazier times. Not that we haven't already experienced some of the most bizarre and crazy times in the last couple years. I don't believe anyone will be able to predict what will come next.

Throughout this chapter, I have brought a lot of discouraging subjects, ideologies, facts, lies, and truths to the surface, so that light can shine upon them. The darkness hates the light because its motives and evil will be exposed. There are *many* who have been deceived by the trickery of Satan. Fallen for the lies and selfish motivations he proclaims will be given. And just as Jesus prophesied two thousand years ago, and so it will be.

> No one knows about that day or hour, not even the angels in heaven, nor the Son, but only the Father. As it was in the days of Noah, so it will be at the coming of the Son of Man. For in the days before the flood, people were eating and drinking, marrying and giving in marriage, up to the day Noah entered the ark; and they knew

> nothing about what would happen until the flood came and took them all away. That is how it will be at the coming of the Son of Man. Two men will be in the field; one will be taken and the other left. Two women will be grinding with a hand mill; one will be taken and the other left.
>
> Therefore, keep watch, because you do not know on what day your Lord will come. But understand this: If the owner of the house had known at what time of night the thief was coming, he would have kept watch and would not have let his house be broken into. So, you also must be ready, because the Son of Man will come at an hour you do not expect him. (Jesus, Matthew 24:36–44)

I don't know about you, but I will be ready. Nothing in this world is going to stop me from being ready, either from rising up in the air to meet him or, in my death, I will rise up to meet him. I am ready.

The Bible gives us plenty of warning to prepare us not only for the troubles that life brings but for what awaits us when we choose to follow Christ. It is a military about face to the world. It is turning your back on the world and your face toward Jesus. It is choosing to please God and not man. Man is fallible, broken, selfish, greedy, messed up, and in the process of choosing the world, it will mess you up and you will be lying face down in a mud puddle, wondering how the heck you ended up there.

> What fools are they who, for a drop of pleasure, drink a sea of wrath. (Unknown)

> Until God is enough, nothing else will be. (Unknown)

SURRENDER

> For He has rescued us from the dominion of darkness and brought us into the Kingdom of the Son he loves, in whom we have redemption, the forgiveness of sins. (Paul, Colossians 1:13–14)

Katharine Hepburn's childhood, in her own words:

> Once when I was a teenager, my father and I were standing in line to buy tickets for the circus.
>
> Finally, there was only one other family between us and the ticket counter. This family made a big impression on me.
>
> There were eight children, all probably under the age of 12. The way they were dressed, you could tell they didn't have a lot of money, but their clothes were neat and clean. The children were well-behaved, all of them standing in line, two-by-two behind their parents, holding hands. They were excitedly jabbering about the clowns, animals, and all the acts they would be seeing that night. By their excitement you could sense they had never been to the circus before. It would be the highlight of their lives.
>
> The father and mother were at the head of the pack standing as proud as can be. The mother was holding her husband's hand, looking up at him as if to say, "You're my knight in shining armor." He was smiling and enjoying seeing his family happy.
>
> The ticket lady asked the man how many tickets he wanted? He proudly responded, "I'd like to buy eight children's tickets and two adult tickets, so I can take my family to the circus." The ticket lady stated the price. The man's wife let go of his hand, her head dropped, the man's lip began to quiver. Then he leaned a little closer

and asked, "How much did you say?" The ticket lady again stated the price.

The man didn't have enough money. How was he supposed to turn and tell his eight kids that he didn't have enough money to take them to the circus? Seeing what was going on, my dad reached into his pocket, pulled out a $20 bill, and then dropped it on the ground. (We were not wealthy in any sense of the word!) My father bent down, picked up the $20 bill, tapped the man on the shoulder and said, "Excuse me, sir, this fell out of your pocket."

The man understood what was going on. He wasn't begging for a handout but certainly appreciated the help in a desperate, heartbreaking and embarrassing situation. He looked straight into my dad's eyes, took my dad's hand in both of his, squeezed tightly onto the $20 bill, and with his lip quivering and a tear streaming down his cheek, he replied, "Thank you, thank you, sir. This really means a lot to me and my family."

My father and I went back to our car and drove home. The $20 that my dad gave away is what we were going to buy our own tickets with. Although we didn't get to see the circus that night, we both felt a joy inside us that was far greater than seeing the circus could ever provide.

That day I learnt the value to Give.

The Giver is bigger than the Receiver. If you want to be large, larger than life, learn to Give. Love has nothing to do with what you are expecting to get—only with what you are expecting to give—which is everything. The importance of giving, blessing others can never be overemphasized because there's always joy in

SURRENDER

giving. Learn to make someone happy by acts of giving. (Katherine Hepburn)

If you never give God a try, you will never know how truly blessed you could be but even more important is what comes after this world is done and over. Eternity is a long time. Choose wisely.

"We will *never* change the world…by going to church. We will only change the world…by *being* the church!"

CHAPTER 4

Pew Warmer

> Morality may keep you out of jail, but it takes the blood of Jesus Christ to keep you out of hell.
> —Charles Spurgeon

> The number one cause of atheism is…Christians. Those who proclaim Him with their mouths and deny Him with their actions is what an unbelieving world finds…simply unbelievable.
> —Karl Rahner, SJ

> Christianity, if false, is of no importance, and if true, of infinite importance. The only thing it cannot be…is moderately important.
> —C. S. Lewis

Explaining this chapter's subject without offending someone is going to be difficult. You might want to leave your feelings at the door. Wish me luck.

I will be honest from the get-go, one of the things I have been challenged with throughout my journey as a Christian is seeing and experiencing someone live out a false faith or what is better known as a pew warmer. Kind of like a bench warmer but sitting in a pew. I recognize that most churches don't even have pews anymore, but it fits the bill. And just to be clear this is not the pew-pew that you hear in Star Wars when storm troopers miss everything they are shooting at.

Now let me try and start off by saying that it is not my intention to offend anyone or even come off judgmental. My true intention is to bring into the light biblically sound doctrine to provide a clearer picture of how we should be living out our faith in Christ.

I believe that if there is anything that we, as believers, are hoping to accomplish, it is to be right with God. We should all want to know Jesus deeply and personally and that our relationship with him should be number one in our life, above all other relationships, above all other things. You know the thing, the "no other gods before me" thing.

Red Letters

As I open the Bible to Matthew, I am instantly drawn to the first red letters that come popping off the page. And here is what I read without reading any of the other correspondence around these red letters:

> Chapter 4, verse 4: "Jesus answered, 'It is written: Man does not live on bread alone, but on every word that comes from the mouth of God.'"
>
> Verse 7: "Jesus answered him, 'It is also written: Do not put the Lord your God to the test.'"
>
> And verse 10: "Jesus said to him, 'Away from me, Satan!' For it is written: 'Worship the Lord your God and serve Him only.'"

Just in these first three red-letter verses, it is clear how much Jesus wants us to be in deep relationship with God. We are to live on every word that comes from the mouth of God. We are told to not put the Lord our God to the test and to worship the Lord and serve him only.

If we were to take these verses literally and live out our lives in faith and action, it would drastically change many people's lives.

But only if we choose to follow and obey, and then, in the process, become a doer of the Word and not attempt to pacify God. But isn't this what many try and do?

We read God's Word, we believe God's Word, we listen to our pastor teach about God's Word, we even do Bible studies and study God's Word. But do we *do* God's Word? Are we doing what is being asked of us? Are we diving in, going deep, seeking out the wholehearted truth, the way, and the life of Jesus?

This is what I want to touch base on.

There is written, or once was written, above the door leading out of our church this message: "You are now entering your mission field." Sadly, I believe it has been painted over.

I am not going to lie and say that I didn't wonder how many people truly lived out this saying because I did, but I also actually wondered how many people read it and chose to ignore it. Because let's be real, when you choose to step into your mission field, this means work and most likely hard work. And Sundays are usually Sabbath days or football watching days or mow the lawn days or take your kids to soccer game days or work in the garden pulling weeds days, etc.

I get it. I have had the privilege and honor to raise four children, two of which are at home, still in school. Well, high school–aged children. You get what I mean.

Life is exhausting. Chores need to be done. Family time is a must. And date nights with the spouse are an absolute must. And to be even more clear, our mission field starts in the home, but it should not end there.

How easy is it to let the things of the world consume us to the point where we have nothing left to offer beyond our own family? Very easy is the answer. So how do you change that? You make it your mission to branch out and schedule events where you can bring the family along so that they can also get a taste of what it means to live out your faith and not just talk it, but be Jesus to those who are in need of your love, your generosity, your time and talents, and to be the light and salt that so many desperately need.

It *has* to become a priority over what this world deems as important. And we *must* be cognizant of how much the world will try and take you out of something as important as this.

Even if you volunteer an hour or two a week at a local Christian based nonprofit thrift store (hint, hint), that would fall under this umbrella of being a doer of the Word and not just a spectator. Participate in serving at a food bank. Mow your elderly neighbor's lawn. *Serve one another.* We are called to be the light in others' lives, not just to go to church and check a box.

> You are part of a puzzle in someone's life. You may never know where you fit. But someone's life may never be complete without you in it. (TobyMac, #speaklife)

Continuing down the line of red letters, let's see where Jesus takes us next, shall we? Chapter 4, verse 19: "'Come and follow me,' Jesus said, 'and I will make you fishers of men.'"

Hmmm, fishers of men you say? So would that be referring to us as well or only to the disciples, for some of them were fisherman?

That was a trick question. I hope you got it right. LOL. Jesus makes it very clear in Matthew 28:18–20 in the Great Commission, "Then Jesus came to them and said, 'All authority in heaven and on earth has been given to me. Therefore, go and make disciples of all nations, baptizing them in the name of the Father and of the Son and of the Holy Spirit, and teaching them to obey everything I have commanded you. And surely I am with you always, to the very end of the age.'"

If this truth is making you squirm and you are contemplating skipping this chapter, I strongly suggest that you don't. Jesus is trying to tell you something. And hopefully, I am helping in the process.

Let me shine some light on something that was said in this last round of verses. In verse 20, Jesus says to teach them to "obey everything I have commanded you." This is something that, for whatever reason, seems unseen or is not picked up on or is simply skimmed over and believed not to be exactly what it says. We are directed to

SURRENDER

obey everything which Jesus commanded the disciples to do. Is that right? Well, that is how I read it. So let's discuss this for a moment. If we were to go back throughout the book of Matthew and read what it was that Jesus commanded them, what would that look like?

Even more important, do you know what is written in the book of Matthew? Have you read the book of Matthew? If not, why not? Do you know who Matthew is in the context of the author? These are all important questions to ask yourself. Because let's be totally transparent here, our Bible reading, our literal time with God, is absolutely imperative to knowing and growing in Jesus. You cannot grow and know who Jesus is without diving deep into the scriptures which are our eternity-determining lifeline to help us get through this thing called life. The scriptures are our lifeline! Prayer is also a must. How else will we communicate with God?

> Prayer is more than a wish; it is the voice of faith directed to God. #kutless

Let's evaluate, for a moment, how many commandments there are from Jesus in just the book of Matthew. Now, I am going to Google that question and see what I come up with. According to Google, Jesus referenced eight commandments, seven from the ten commandments, and the one Jesus added which is to love your neighbor as yourself as the second greatest commandment after the first and greatest commandment which is to "Love the Lord your God with all your heart and with all your soul and with all your mind."

What I have to ask though is this: there are many other commands that Jesus put forth to his disciples that are outside of the ten commandments, is he referring to these also? I would say 100 percent yes! Therefore, Jesus's words, his parables, the red letters are *all paramount* to how we choose to obey our Lord and Savior. How we choose to obey his commands. How we choose to apply them to our lives and use them, live them out so that they become a part of who we are, which is a new creation in Christ Jesus.

God's Word should excite you, lift you up and fill you up and enlighten you to a much deeper understanding of our place in this world. To those of us who have been chosen, our purpose here is deeper and greater than we can ever imagine.

> We are told that Christ was killed for us, that His death has washed away our sins, and that by dying he disabled death itself. That is the formula, that is Christianity, that is what has to be believed. (C. S. Lewis)

So to answer the question, to obey his commands, to be fishers of men, and enter into your mission field means to be all-in for this Jesus fella. It cannot be half and half or 30-70 or 60-40, it should be, and you should want it to be, 100 percent.

Not a pew warmer. Not sitting on the fence until something makes you change your mind. The time is now. There is no time but the present. If the sands of your hourglass end tomorrow, because nobody knows how long they have, wouldn't you want to be ready?

> Always remember, the crowd chose Barabbas—not because they loved him, but because they hated the truth. Now let that sink in. (Anonymous)

The truth is simply that, the truth. It cannot be erased or forgotten, minimized or simply ignored, it must be obeyed. God's truth cannot be watered down, dissected, cherry-picked, just to make it fit into your perfect little box with the purpose of making Jesus smaller than he is or trying to make his word not so powerful or blatantly difficult. We either become a slave to Christ or we become a slave to something else. We either love Jesus or we love the world. We are either one with Jesus or we are of the world. Your choice. But never forget, your choice begets your eternal end result. Your will is yours to choose, and God won't force his will onto you. That is why it is free will.

> Our Bible reading should not be a marathon, but a slow, deliberate soaking in of its message. (A. W. Tozer)

"Practice what you preach," many say, but not as many do. There are many out there full of biblical knowledge and wisdom, but if it stays in the mind and never reaches the heart, that could be trouble. God wants your heart. He wants it to be given to him by us willingly and wholeheartedly. Our mind is just the tool to file away what we need when we need it. But the heart is full of the blood of Jesus when you truly and genuinely ask him into it. His mission is to transform that heart of stone into a heart of flesh filled with love and compassion for others and to love God with all of it.

> If I speak in the tongues of men and of angels, but have not love, I am only a resounding gong or a clanging symbol. If I have the gift of prophecy and can fathom all mysteries and all knowledge, and if I have a faith that can move mountains, but have not love, I am nothing. If I give all I possess to the poor and surrender my body to the flames, but have not love, I gain nothing.
> Love is patient, love is kind, it does not envy, it does not boast, it is not proud. It is not rude, it is not self-seeking, it is not easily angered, it keeps no record of wrongs. Love does not delight in evil but rejoices with the truth. It always protects, always trusts, always hopes, always perseveres.
> Love never fails. (Paul, 1 Corinthians 13:1–8)

Somewhere along the line of Americanized Christianity, we have lost our way. We have seriously made Jesus powerless, and the gospel of Jesus has been so greatly watered down to not offend anyone. The gospel has become a shredded book with many pages slammed with holes and parts cut out so that our selfishness can be fulfilled without guilt or shame. We want our worldly possessions, our sin to be glorified, and our salvation to be easy. Just give me the Willy Wonka Golden Ticket so I can get into heaven, and I will try my best (not really) to live as morally possible as I can be. I am a good person, and I am nice to everyone; therefore, I am a shoo-in to get into heaven. For sure!

Pew warmer.

You either get right with God or you don't. You either get taken when Jesus comes back to take us up to heaven with him or you get left behind. You either die and go to heaven or you die and go to hell. This is just the facts, ma'am. (That was my Dragnet impression.)

> For the Lord himself will come down from heaven, with a loud command, with the voice of the archangel and with the trumpet call of God, and the dead in Christ will rise first. After that, we who are still alive and are left will be caught up together with them in the clouds to meet the Lord in the air. And so we will be with the Lord forever. Therefore encourage each other with these words. (Paul, 1 Thessalonians 4:16–18)

Seriously though, which is it? How much weight do you put into this truth? I can quote and write down verse after verse sealing a win in my case for Christ which would be air-tight and rock-solid, but I am not sure that is necessary.

> And you will be hated by all nations because of me. (Jesus, Matthew 24:9)

SURRENDER

Death, persecution, suffering, martyred...these are all the descriptions that Jesus tells us will be handed down to us if we choose to follow him. Jesus demands that if we are to follow him, then we *must* pick up our cross daily and deny ourselves. Basically dying to oneself. This is the true calling of those who have been called and chosen by Jesus. That is a hard pill to swallow. And *that* might be why some choose not to go any further than a pew warmer. Is it worth the cost and sacrifice? Is it worth it to suffer as Christ suffered? Was it worth the cost and sacrifice when Jesus died for you and me?

Was it worth it for him to deny himself, suffer excruciating pain, being rejected and despised by his own people, spat upon, beaten, tortured, whipped with thirty-nine lashes that tore into skin, muscle, and tissue straight to the bone? Was it worth it to him to have nine-inch nails hammered through his wrists, through cartilage, muscle, and bone or to have those same nails hammered through both feet? Was it?

Did we deserve that kind of love—any of us? Do we still? Nope. Not a lick of forgiveness. But Jesus did this for us anyway, and I think we might owe him something even though his salvation is a gift he gave us *for free*.

> Insecurity wants to keep track of our failures. Grace doesn't even write them down. (Bob Goff)

> But thanks be to God! He gives us the victory through our Lord Jesus Christ. (Paul, 1 Corinthians 15:57)

It all comes down to a choice; every day, choices are made. What will you choose? Who will you choose?

I am far from perfect, through Christ, a beautiful mess. I fail every day. I fall every day, but the grace of Jesus picks me back up every time. *Every time.* If we rely on our own understanding, our own strength, we will not only fail, but fall into the darkness of hell where there will be weeping and gnashing of teeth. If we choose the world instead of Jesus, expect not only hell on earth, but hell eternal. I don't think you want me to pull out scripture describing what many are experiencing right now and what many more will be in the future in the depths of darkness with no reprieve from an eternal place that will be filled with void and never-ending turmoil.

Wake up, people! It is time to wake up! Look up, stand up, and worship the Lord who loves you so much! It is time to get right with God, enter into your purpose, enter into your mission field whatever that may be and leave the pew *cold*. Heck, let's set the pew on fire. You won't be needing it anymore!

> If we find ourselves with a desire that nothing in this world can satisfy, the most probable explanation is that we were made for another world. (C. S. Lewis)

> May God give you grace to see sin as it really is in His sight, for then you will realize your need of a Savior. (Charles Spurgeon)

I have said it before, and I will say it again: be a doer of the Word. Make sure Jesus finds you working out your salvation with fear and trembling! Stand up and praise God for there is much to praise him for. Be the light and salt of Jesus in living out your faith as fishers of men and women. This is precious in his sight. Jesus loves the little children of the world!

Amen. Thank you, Jesus.

> The absence of the concept of discipleship from present-day Christianity leaves a vacuum which we instinctively try to fill with one or another substitute. I name a few. Pietism. By this I mean…an enjoyable feeling of affection for the person of our Lord which is valued for itself and is wholly unrelated to cross-bearing or the keeping of the commandments of Christ.

SURRENDER

It is entirely possible to feel for Jesus an ardent love which is not of the Holy Spirit. Witness the love for the Virgin felt by certain devout souls, a love which in the very nature of things must be purely subjective. The heart is adept at emotional tricks and is entirely capable of falling in love with imaginary objects or romantic religious ideas.

In the confused world of romance…young persons are constantly inquiring how they can tell when they are in love. They are afraid they may mistake some other sensation for true love and are seeking some trustworthy criterion by which they can judge the quality of their latest emotional fever. Their confusion of course arises from the erroneous notion that love is an enjoyable inward passion, without intellectual or volitional qualities and carrying with it no moral obligations.

Our Lord gave us a rule by which we can test our love for Him: "Whoever has my commands and obeys them, he is the one who loves me. He who loves me will be loved by my Father, and I too will love him and show myself to him." Then Judas (not Judas Iscariot) said, "But, Lord, why do you intend to show yourself to us and not to the world?"

Jesus replied, "If anyone loves me, he will obey my teaching. My Father will love him, and we will come to him and make our home with him. He who does not love me will not obey my teaching. These words you hear are not my own; they belong to the Father who sent me." (John 14:21–24)

These words are too plain to need much interpreting. Proof of love for Christ is simply removed altogether from the realm of the feelings and placed in the realm of practical obedience. I think the rest of the New Testament is in full accord with this. (A. W. Tozer, *Loving Obedience*)

A man who lies to himself, and believes his own lies becomes
unable to recognize truth, either in himself or anyone else,
and he ends up losing respect for himself and for others.
When he has no respect for anyone, he can no longer love,
and, in order to divert himself, having no love in him,
he yields to his impulses, indulges in the lowest forms
of pleasure, and behaves in the end like an animal.
And it all comes from lying—lying to others and to yourself.

—Fyodor Dostoevsky

CHAPTER 5

Lose so You Can Win

Christians have nothing to be smug about; we are not righteous people trying to correct the unrighteous. As one preacher said, "Evangelism is just one beggar telling the other beggar where to find bread." The chief difference between the believer and the unbeliever is forgiveness.
—R. C. Sproul

There is only one middleman between us and God… and it is not the Pope, a pastor, a priest, or a prophet. It is Jesus.
—Anonymous

"You know…I think one of the most interesting verses in the New Testament is when Peter tells the church, *"Insofar as it is possible live at peace with all men."* You know…that insofar as it is possible—that indicates the variability of circumstances. And we're in a situation right now where just to be a believing Christian you're going to be charged with being an oppressor, you know. Complicit with the oppressor state. You're going to be accused of being homophobic and transphobic. And even to use the language right now…Islamophobic and all the rest. So, if you're phobic about being called phobic… you're going to be in a big, big problem. And so, I think part of what this generation has to do is just understand, look, insofar as it is possible, we are going to live at

SURRENDER

peace with all men. And in a lot of situations that's not as possible as we would like. And so, Peter didn't make that unconditional, it's actually conditional. *"Insofar as it is possible."* And so…I want young Christians to be as winsome, as joyful, as kind, as gracious as possible. But to stand as firmly, as boldly, as courageous and indeed as costly as is necessary for Christian faithfulness.

—Unknown

As many of you already know and to those who don't, my wife and I opened a nonprofit thrift store in historic downtown Snoqualmie, Washington, around two and half years ago (2021). It is a beautiful little town with its vintage original train depot and many old trains that still run and give rides to and from our neighboring city of North Bend and then to the main local attraction of Snoqualmie Falls. On most weekends, you can hear the deep bellowing whistle from the steam train locomotive as it is either leaving or returning to the depot.

It has been a blessing growing up here in a town once known for being a hick town, with cow milking, tree logging, and beautiful Mount Si as our backdrop. A lot has changed over the course of forty-plus years. Since the booming headquarters of Amazon, Starbucks, Microsoft, and Boeing being in our state, the consumerism money drifted in and came to touch this once small valley where it seemed nearly everyone was related.

When I graduated high school from Mount Si High, jokingly referred to then as Cow-Pie High, we had maybe 120 graduating seniors. Now they have over 1,200. That might be a bit of an exaggeration, but it is close. The high school I went to is no longer there. They demolished it and built a brand-new one twice the size of the last one. It is now the biggest high school in the state, which looks and feels like a community college. Crazy.

In our thrift store, we see many walks of life and many different characters. It is a very diverse set of people from the homeless to the rich. And with that bit of info, you can only imagine the challenge we face to be as flexible and patient with the variety of crayons we deal with on a daily basis. Luckily, I have only had to kick out two people in the 2.5 years since we have been open. But for the most part, it has been quite a lovely experience.

For those of you who don't know, let me give you a little peek behind the curtain as to how we make this store stay alive and succeed as each day brings about new challenges to serve the people.

Without going too deep into the full story which I have already written in the last book I wrote, faithfully, I simply want to shine a light on this example so as to tie in the true understanding of what it means to surrender, what it means to lose, so you can win.

Too often, the temptation of the many things in this world become more important to people, and with that choice comes an even deeper feeling of loss and emptiness.

One of the main staples of our business is in the reliance on donations from people in our community. Maybe they no longer care to hold on to the possessions they have or they have been put in a position where an overabundance of items have become theirs is the result of a death in the family. Sometimes, a loved one has had to be moved into a care facility, or they are simply moving and no longer want the things they have, so they would like to donate them. Whatever the reason may be, in their generosity, we are then called upon to either drive our seventeen-foot U-Haul, properly named Jabba the Truck, to their residence and pick through years and years of someone's accumulation of stuff or they bring it to our store, and we happily pick through it there.

And when I say pick, I am literally picking and choosing only what I believe we have a shot at selling. After doing this now for over ten years and being a thrift store/yard sale junkie myself, it is ingrained into my brain what has value and what does not. I am certainly not an expert, but I do believe this is one of the gifts God has given me. Otherwise, I don't think I would have been chosen for a task such as this.

But I am humbled and grateful for the opportunity I have been gifted with to be able to serve and love so many people who are either giving or purchasing for this mission.

One of the craziest things to watch and see is the changing season of items that are popular one day and then become unwanted the next. There will be certain items that I cannot keep on the shelf, and then a few months later, nobody wants them anymore. This is not abnormal because we all know there are fads and waves of collectibles or antiques that for whatever reason become sought after one day and then, nope, not anymore.

With the craziness of the store, at times, it can get a bit overwhelming, but I am beginning to see that the story of our store is finally reaching and touching the hearts of many people in our valley and beyond.

When I received the vision from God to open a nonprofit thrift store, I instantly shared it with my wife and because of her and the gifts that God had given her, we became the Wonder Twins and believed wholeheartedly and with tremendous faith that with God's help, we can do this. Wonder Twin powers, *activate*!

Form of servants of God to love and serve the people all the while pointing *not* to us for the glory, but to the only One who deserves all the Glory. (Side note: For those not old enough to know who the Wonder Twins are, they were created and added into the Super Friends cartoon of the '70s which included Superman, Batman, Wonder Woman, etc. Make sure you Google them to get the full experience of this paragraph.)

Without God, there is no thrift store.

Without God, this man, who was extremely broken, would not be healed. Without God, there would be no calling, no purpose.

Without God, over one hundred clean water wells would not have been built in Uganda serving thousands and thousands of people and saving thousands more from an early death.

Without God, *so* many more families in need would not get the food they need, the shelter, the tents, the sleeping bags and blankets, clothes, and so many other needs that would just be left unmet.

Without God, we wouldn't be able to give and do so much and offer love to those who so desperately need to be loved.

Without God, I wouldn't be writing this book, and you wouldn't be reading it. Without God, fill in the blank.

> Without love, there is no reason to know
> anyone, for love will, in the end, connect us

> to our neighbors, our children and our hearts.
> (Martin Luther King Jr.)

I choose to *lose* this life for the sake of Jesus Christ, so I can win the race and receive the prize.

There is *nothing* more important than this.

Trust me, please trust me in knowing this. There are days when I want to run. I want to walk away and never look back. In choosing to lose, which is really winning, is choosing to let go of it all. To let go of that which you believe is yours. To let go of your time, to let go of your selfishness, to let go of your possessions, your dreams, your ideas of what you believe is going to make you happy. You must let go and give it all away. In doing so, you are putting *all of your faith* into the One who knows what is best for you and *trusting* in that choice that if you step off this cliff, God will provide a bridge to close the chasm between our mustard seed faith and the arms of our loving Savior.

The crazy thing is this: when we let go, truly let go, *then* (and only then) can God move. Our will has to be his will. It's nonnegotiable. We have to lose to win! And in losing, we end up gaining tenfold of what we chose to let go of. This is my experience, and I would never change a thing about it.

> Do not be deceived: God cannot be mocked. A man reaps what he sows. The one who sows to please his sinful nature, from that nature will reap destruction; the one who sows to please the Spirit, from the Spirit will reap eternal life. Let us not become weary in doing good, for at the proper time we will reap a harvest if we do not give up. Therefore, as we have opportunity, let us do good to all people, especially to those who belong to the family of believers. (Paul, Galatians 6:7–10)

SURRENDER

In our store, we have seen and experienced many amazing and heartfelt stories that take place on almost a daily basis. I try and share as many as I can because of the importance of knowing how many lives, how many hearts, and how many souls are being touched, cared for, and moved to tears because of the sacrificial acts of love being given through the process of this nonprofit mission.

There are also many events and stories that I don't share because then it seems more like boasting than it does to give glory to God. The most important premise in the process of building our faith-based store has been the intention, as it should be, to point to the One who deserves it.

> There is a rare breed of people who go all in. They keep their word. They give it their all. They put themselves last for those they care about. These individuals rarely receive the same compassion and effort in return yet continue to give freely. To the givers, forgivers and selfless lovers out there…keep pushing forward. Don't let this cold world change who you are. (Unknown)

I will never forget when our church had a guest speaker by the name of Brendan Manning. He was an amazing man and had written many books that I have read, which helped me to see the importance of living a life of humility in words and actions. When he came to speak, he had to be close to eighty years old. And when he was done speaking, we all stood to applaud him. He humbly turned around on the stage with his back to us and pointed up to the One who had done it all.

If you have not read his book, *The Ragamuffin Gospel*, I highly recommend it.

> But because of His great love for us, God, who is rich in mercy, made us alive with Christ even when we were dead in transgressions—it is by grace you have been saved. And God raised us

up with Christ and seated us up with Him in the heavenly realms in Christ Jesus, in order that in the coming ages He might show the incomparable riches of His grace, expressed in His kindness to us in Christ Jesus.

For it is by grace you have been saved, through faith—and this not from yourselves, it is the gift of God—not by works, so that no one can boast. For we are God's workmanship, created in Christ Jesus to do good works, which God prepared in advance for us to do. (Paul, Ephesians 2:4–10)

There is no greater love than to lay down one's life for one's friends. (Jesus, John 15:13)

The sacrificial act of love is in the action of the one who loves and steps forward to fulfill that action without remorse or to believe that his/her actions will be reimbursed. We must understand this and move in the direction of Christ so we may love those who need our love. We only get so many chances in this life.

Choose wisely; seek out Jesus with all your heart and do your best to emulate him.

A couple of weeks ago, a woman walked into the store and found a small item to purchase. She then proceeded to tell me that she would like to make a cash donation as well. I rang up her small item and then she informed me that she would like to donate $500!

I lost it. I cried like a baby. I had no words.

Her one act of kindness reverberated through me to my very soul, and it filled my heart with her love—her choice to give from a place of pure love. I could not hold back the tears. I came out from behind the register and gave her a big hug and thanked her for her kindness and her generosity.

When you are pouring into something, giving it everything you have to make as much money as you can so you can give it away, working endless hours to present a stocked store to your community with blood, sweat, and tears, a gift like this brings you to your knees. It is a huge breath of clean, crisp air. It is a love that hits deep within your core, and it is good.

My true intention, my goal and my dream, has always been to lose so I can win.

> What good will it be for someone to gain the whole world, yet forfeit their soul? Or what can anyone give in exchange for their soul? (Jesus, Matthew 16:26)

> And anyone who does not take up their cross and follow me is not worthy of me. Whoever finds his life will lose it, and whoever loses his life for my sake will find it. (Jesus, Matthew 10:38–39)

I guarantee you this, there is *no greater* feeling in the world than to give from your heart in the willingness to bring joy to someone who is in great need of your gift. Even if it is your time, to lend an ear, a hug, or a simple task, these will mean more to someone than we will ever know.

A pebble thrown into a lake of glass leaves thousands of ripples that can affect many in its wake. I want to be that pebble.

Stories from a Thrift Store

One of my favorite and most precious treasures that I am honored to be a part of is to *give* to those who walk in our store who have nothing yet are so desperate for the simple things the rest of us can take for granted.

I knew that this store would be special, but I had no idea to the lengths and depths of giving we would be able to provide or how many souls we would be able to touch. We have one homeless gentleman who comes in our store and is usually drunk or high on something who is in great need of clothing or shoes or both. I never hesitate to offer what we have and simply allow him to go and get whatever he needs. When he is done gathering a few pairs of pants, a couple sweatshirts, and a pair of shoes, he always says with a tear in his eye, "Thank you so much" and ends it with an "I love you, Don." Which then I reply, "I love you too, Al."

Through the stench of alcohol and dirty clothes, this small act of kindness is seen clearly and felt deeply with so much gratitude from this downtrodden old man that he accepts the gift with great appreciation and love. He knows this is from the heart. And to see our homeless customers come in, know they are welcome as they are, and to recognize the appreciation they feel when they are gifted with whatever they need is powerful. Every single one of them knows they can come and ask, and we will look them in the eye and tell them they are loved and help them supply their needs. Sometimes, they even try to pay, but we will not let them.

I have a hundred more stories like this, and these kinds of stories happen every day. But the most important part of this story that I want to make transparent and understandable is this: each and every choice we make every day is either wrapped in a bow, a gift from the heart, or it is suffocating with selfish intentions that will be expected to be repaid one way or the other.

If your heart is cold, then the gift is intentionally given for others to see so you get the credit for it. If your heart is warm and loving and the gift is given as an act of love, then the gift is given from a heart overflowing with love for your neighbor or a perfect stranger.

This is the most important part of giving. Your treasures are trash if it is given with a selfish heart and with selfish ambitions so that you may receive compliments on your giving or be held in great regard with accolades, awards, and applause.

God knows your heart.

One of the hardest things I struggle with almost daily is when a proclaiming Christian, who is not struggling for anything, haggles me for every penny that they are spending on items in our store when we offer our items at well below wholesale cost. Something for which they would easily have to spend three to four times as much at a regular store, and they want it for next to nothing when they absolutely know for a fact where the money is going. I literally have to turn over my shoulder to point to a large picture of African children with a clear plastic water bottle filled with brown, disgusting, diseased, drinking water and remind them that the money from these graciously donated items are going to save children just like this with clean water wells and to the homeless in our communities, local food banks, and to help with teens who are struggling.

I am afraid for people like this because one day, they will have to stand before Jesus and answer the question: "Why didn't you give this child a drink of clean water?"

> And the King will reply, "Truly I tell you, whatever you did for the least of these brothers and sisters of mine, you did for me."
>
> Then He will say to those on His left, "Depart from me, you who are cursed, into the eternal fire prepared for the devil and his angels. For I was hungry and you gave me nothing to eat, I was thirsty and you gave me nothing to drink, I was a stranger and you did not invite me in, I needed clothes and you did not clothe me, I was sick and in prison and you did not look after me."
>
> They also will answer, "Lord, when did we see you hungry or thirsty or a stranger or needing clothes or sick or in prison, and did not help you?"
>
> He will reply, "Truly I tell you, whatever you *did not* do for one of the least of these, you *did not* do for me." (Jesus, Matthew 25:40–45 [emphasis mine])

Warning after warning after warning. But do we listen and obey? Do we take the words of Jesus literally? Or do we sugarcoat them, skim over these passages, and pretend that this does not apply to us?

"Jesus loves me and would never throw me into hell. I am a good person with high morals and follow the commandments." Sorry, folks, this is not what he has told us.

Wake *up*! The time is near. Please understand, I am not the judge and jury here. I am simply the messenger. I am making known what is evident and clear, hoping to *wake people up* to the truth and prepare them for what is to come, either in this life or the eternal life to come.

Lose so you can win! Those who are last will be first and the first, last. In the eyes of the world, they tell you to be first.

> If you ain't first…You're last! (Ricky Bobby, *Talladega Nights*)

Jesus is trying to help us to understand that to be a winner in the eyes of Christ is to humble yourself before others, putting their needs above your own. When you're last intentionally for others' sake, for the sake of Jesus, you will be first in the kingdom of heaven. You lose; therefore, you win.

There is no end to the battle over the soul; until our bodies can no longer live, then the soul is set free. Unless of course, Jesus comes back. Which would be intense and amazing. Unless you're left behind, and that is not an option for me. Unless of course, Jesus has other plans in mind for me to remain on earth as a tribulation saint, bringing many more souls to Jesus.

It is inevitable; like I said before, none of us is getting out of here alive. Our time on this earth is but a blip. You only have so many days, so many years, and then the clock stops ticking.

Today, now, is when we all need to look in the mirror. Ask yourself, ask God, "How am I doing?" If you asked that honestly, be prepared to hear the truth. If you do not hear God, then you better go looking for him. Take an honest inventory of who you are. Do not sugarcoat it or water it down; be honest with yourself. How am I doing according to God's Word?

This *is* the most important choice you will ever make.

SURRENDER

Ego vs. Soul
(Malaena Mae Horst Willhite, #AngelMinute)

Ego seeks to serve itself; Soul seeks to serve others.
Ego seeks outward recognition; Soul seeks inner authenticity.
Ego sees life as a competition; Soul sees life as a gift.
Ego seeks to preserve self; Soul seeks to preserve others.
Ego looks outward; Soul looks inward.
Ego feels lack; Soul feels abundance.
Ego is mortal; Soul is eternal.
Ego is drawn to lust; Soul is drawn to love.
Ego seeks wisdom; Soul is wisdom.
Ego enjoys the prize; Soul enjoys the journey.
Ego is cause of pain; Soul is cause of healing.
Ego rejects God, Soul embraces God.
Ego is Me; Soul is We.

This generation has forgotten that the Gospel message does not clean up and shine the outside of a person. Rather it bores into the very heart and soul of a person and radically changes that person from the inside forever. (A. W. Tozer, *A Man of God*)

Everything else is worthless when compared with the infinite value of knowing Christ Jesus my Lord. (Paul, Philippians 3:8)

If you are Christians, be consistent. Be Christians out and out; Christians every hour, in every part. Beware of halfhearted discipleship, of compromise with evil, of conformity to the world, of trying to serve two masters—to walk in two ways, the narrow and the broad, at once. It will not do. Halfhearted Christianity will only dishonor God, while it makes you miserable.

—Horatius Bonar, 1872

CHAPTER 6

Who Am I?

The beginning of love is the will to let those we love be perfectly themselves, the resolution not to twist them to fit our own image. If in loving them we do not love what they are, but only their potential likeness to ourselves, then we do not love them: we only love the reflection of ourselves we find in them.
—Thomas Merton

Some people will never like you…because
your spirit irritates their demons.
—Denzel Washington

This road I will be attempting to travel down could very much be…a slippery slope. So therefore…I will do my best to travel softly and lightly…while I throw down some cat litter and ice melt here and there for traction.

Indeed…five lies of our Anti-Christian age have coiled their way from the world to the church, and I have nothing to stand on. I used to believe all of these lies once. And what are the five lies? Well…we just covered one of them…Homosexuality is normal. The second lie is that pagan spirituality is kind and inclusive. The third lie is that feminism is good for the church and the world. The fourth lie is that Transgenderism is normal. And the fifth lie is that modesty for women is outdated and dangerous.

These lies which have entered the church and the Christian college have one thing in common. They discourage repentance of sin, and they encourage the pride of victimhood. You see, the Bible throws no one away and neither should Christians. But the Bible sets the terms of God's blessing. God cannot be mocked.

—Dr. Rosaria Butterfield

It never ceases to amaze me to what depths our Western society, which has now become the entire world society, clings on to and scratches its way to—whatever is the most popular, central message so blaringly and blatantly being shouted out from every corner of the globe and from every mountaintop as far as the eye can see and the ear can hear.

Right this very minute, all across the world and in our own country, the United States, there are so many major universities praising the violence, brutality, and bloodshed viciously done from the terrorist group, Hamas, in the killing of over 1,200 Jews. And not just from young adults in universities, but parades of people, thousands of people, marching down major cities all over the world, praising these horrendous attacks on innocent babies, children, wives, husbands, grandparents. Horrendous acts that I will not even write down in this book. Over 200 taken hostage; too many women and children brutally raped and killed.

Unthinkable brutality and yet people are flocking in to follow what is new and exciting to blatantly abuse and promote without a single clue as to what they are promoting and praising without pause for verification of information. Sickening and so terribly sad.

In our world these days, if something happens in Billingsley, Alabama, it will be seen and heard in Athens, Greece, and Semarang, Singapore, almost immediately.

Whatever happens in Nagasaki, Japan, will be seen and heard in Helena, Montana, and Vallenar, Chile. Our world is a very small place now. Our TV screens no longer weigh 500 pounds and once where there was only 3 channels and a set of rabbit ears wrapped in aluminum foil, we now have, according to Statista, in 2021, over 15 billion television screens all over the world in the form of cell phone mobile devices.

Anything that even becomes remotely popular or trendy is instantly spread like wildfire throughout many different nationalities, countries, and cities all over the world in seconds. Not only are we not alone, but we are all intricately connected scientifically, emotionally, physically, spiritually, and electronically.

Never in the history of the world have we been this connected to the point of instantly having video feed with volume from Snoqualmie, Washington, to Kampala, Uganda, in a matter of seconds. Fascinating and scary. When my wife was on her last military deployment to Qatar, we were able to video call *twice a day* every day with ease! On all of her previous deployments, she would have to wait in the queue for a fifteen-minute call on voice over internet protocol shared phone lines in a community center! When our fathers were serving in Thailand and Vietnam, they just had to wait for letters—and they waited a long time for every single one. We don't even wait that long for something we order on Amazon! We live in an age of instant gratification and instant distraction.

To this effect, we have become one. And when the world ebbs and flows, we all dance to the rolling movement. But this we know for sure: the world is ever changing and ever evolving, constantly going with the flow or changing the fashion or whatever is popular of so many different beliefs, fads, entertainment choices, whatever is trending, and what and where are people choosing to gravitate?

Everyone is looking for their identity. Everyone is looking for their clan, their club, their gang, and their place in this world. Who am I and who do I want to represent? Who and what do I believe in? What best fits my character, my persona, my image? We live in a world of so many people who are in limbo or who are lost, wanting so badly to feel loved, to feel welcomed and wanted, and to be seen. There are those who so badly just want to have some form of purpose that they will even join and be part of something so terribly wrong.

Those who grew up without a healthy relationship with their dad or mom, those who fought through life with an abusive parent, a parent who was absent or abandoned their child, or a parent who struggled with addiction, the pain and confusion runs deep. That kind of pain, especially sexual abuse, can cause such a dark and negative ripple effect; it can and will affect many, many lives, and it can cause damage in generation after generation after generation. If that pain, if that reality, does not get the proper help it needs, all the while festering and bleeding onto the innocence of others, especially children, then the devil has done his job: he has destroyed life that God created for love.

> Until you heal the wounds of your past, you are going to bleed. You bandage the bleeding with food, with alcohol, with drugs, with work, with cigarettes, with sex; But eventually, it will all ooze through and stain your life. You must find the strength to open the wounds, stick your hands inside, pull out the core of the pain that is holding you in your past, the memories and make peace with them. (Unknown)

A broken tree has many branches, and each year, the branches have many new shoots, and once those trees shed their leaves and seeds, more broken trees and branches grow. After a while, you have a forest filled with broken, twisted, and diseased trees that eventually poison the streams that run into the rivers, and those rivers lead to the ocean which in turn touches every life.

The point is with each new broken generation, this world is poisoned with more evil, sickness, and darkness. A huge number of people are sick, broken, diseased, have a mental illness, and are lost. They are lost because nobody has found them, nobody has truly loved them. So many do not feel loved, worthy, beautiful, accepted; they have been poisoned by a lie that they are not worthy in this world, and they are not worthy of God's love. That is Satan, and he has been working overtime.

So many of them choose an even darker path for their lives and never find truth, love, or the way. Sex, drugs, alcohol, prostitution, pornography, child sex abuse, jailtime, murder, homelessness, child trafficking, greed, addictions, suicide, materialism, domestic violence, etc., etc.—all of these are roads to the dark side of town.

And with that comes great confusion, lies, and temptation—anything to help them to feel loved, important, and wanted.

> If you don't heal what hurt you, you'll bleed
> on people who didn't cut you. (Unknown)

And with all this, all this pain and confusion, mixed with what is the latest trend or popular fad, you end up with a world following after and falling over each other, trying to fit into what makes them feel important, feel seen and heard. And so, the sin grows deeper, and the darkness ever darker. We are seeing the evil of this world manifest itself to become a powerful force affecting every corner and touching every family, leaving everyone wondering what will happen next.

> You will be hated all over the world because you are my followers. And many will turn away from me and betray and hate each other. And many false prophets will appear and will deceive many people. Sin will be rampant everywhere, and the love of many will grow cold. But the one who endures to the end will be saved. And the Good News about the Kingdom will be preached throughout the whole world, so that all nations will hear it; and then the end will come. (Jesus, Matthew 24:9–14)

But this is not the end.
Yes, evil is rampant. But there is a God who is still in control.

> I am the vine; you are the branches. If you remain in me and I in you, you will bear much fruit; *apart from me you can do nothing.* (Jesus, John 15:5 [emphasis mine])

Those who choose to live separated from God on this earth do so willingly, without regard for the consequences of their actions both here on earth and what is to come. *All* of us will be held accountable. All of us.

> They fear love because it creates a world they can't control. (George Orwell, *1984*)

So who am I? Who are you?

Who have you chosen to become or, even more accurately, chosen to represent?

You may *think* you are not representing anyone but yourself, but you are representing someone or something. Everyone has something they worship. Something they follow. Something that has manifested in themselves to help them believe they are something that has worth.

So let's dig a little deeper.

> Never worry about who will be offended if you speak the truth. Worry about who will be misled, deceived and destroyed…if you don't! (TobyMac, #speaklife)

This quote I am about to share with you is powerful in its solid truth of who we were, who God wants us to be, and the process it takes to get there. Read this and then maybe read it again.

> God's commitment to us isn't intended to make us comfortable, but to conform us to the image of His Son. (Romans 8:29) And that process necessitates difficulties. It resembles that of a sculptor who, seeing beauty in a slab of stone, diligently goes to work. Initially great pieces are removed, then the intricate details are chiseled until at last the desired image is revealed.

SURRENDER

> Believer, everything that is happening at this moment is absolute proof of God's continuing work "in" us. Never assume that God is done with you. That work will only be complete when you meet Jesus face-to-face. (Jack Hibbs)

All of us must come to the conclusion of who we have become, of who we have chosen to be, and of whom we have chosen to represent. Nobody else to blame, only you.

And with this grandiose introduction, I hereby move to motion to the next level of absurdity. The next best thing and the next greatest tool of Satan that has become in many ways a popular fad or ideology that is twisted and has flooded every area of our living world: the woke theology.

I will start by saying, I am baffled to no end to the suggestion and twisted idea that men can be women and women, men. To the degree at which none of this makes sense. Not only is this impossible, but scientifically, spiritually, biologically, and physically *impossible*.

You can point to a cow, and it's still easily recognizable that yes, that is still a cow. If it has four udders and you can milk it, it is a cow, which in turn gives birth to baby cows. If you cut off the udders, it is *still* a female cow. I *highly* recommend you do not try and milk a bull and say it is a cow. End of story.

> Stand up for what is right...even if you stand alone. (TobyMac, #speaklife)

This belief, this trend that is flooding the world with this ideocratic ideology in the sense that this is even possible is purely based on feelings and not on facts.

Those who support it and are pushing this ideology are squarely on board simply because of the possibility of someone's feelings being hurt. This does not change the truth of the situation. And this certainly does not mean that because someone says they are a man when they are clearly a woman, that this, in turn, suggests we must also agree with this person's sexual dysphoria? Nope, I don't think so.

> If I say a man is a man and a woman is a woman is inherently transphobic…that's not discrimination…that's disagreement. I have said and I will continue to maintain the gender dysphoria or gender identity disorder, which ever DSM you choose to use, is a mental illness. God forbid that it should be said with any animus because this is not said with animus. When people are suffering…these are clearly folks who are suffering. When people are suffering…you shouldn't be saying stuff with animus. I am not saying that as a…Gotcha!…to people who are transgender… the point that I am making is that when a society begins treating folks who have mental illness as though they are representing an objective reality…they are doing no service to the people who actually suffer from a mental illness. (Ben Shapiro)

Do we love them right where they are? Absolutely. Do we have to agree with them to love them? Absolutely not.

> God is not going to rewrite the Bible for your opinions or your feelings, stop trying to change the scripture when it's written to change you. (Unknown)

> You can sway a thousand men by appealing to their prejudices quicker than you can convince one man by logic. (Robert A. Heinlein)

Many will scream "Bigot!" "Hater!" "Racist!" and that is not even close to the truth. Truth trumps feelings. If we don't stand up to this, then what else? What other nonsense will be pushed into an agenda that must be followed and obeyed?

Gender ideology, gender dysphoria, binary, nonbinary, transgender, homosexuality, woke theology—all of this, believe it or not, falls under the umbrella of sexual sin, and most people either don't want to talk about it or pretend it isn't rampant throughout our world like a virus or wildfire burning down everything in its path. Call it what it is. Biblically, it is all a sin. It goes against everything that God has created in a man and a woman. You can call it anything you want, it is still a sin. Again, does this mean we hate those who practice or believe in this lifestyle? No, it just means we don't agree with it and will not be made to accept it as normal or to be coerced or forced to call people who are men, women or women, men. Nope. Not going to do it.

It is like putting a gorilla in front of me and saying it is a dolphin. You *must* call it a dolphin, treat it like a dolphin, and change how you think of this dolphin because it thinks it is a dolphin or you will hurt its feelings. *So what*! That doesn't change anything. Sorry your feelings are hurt, but that is not my problem.

> If you are silent about your beliefs because you are worried someone will be offended, then your beliefs are not that important to you, but rather what people think about you is. When you stand up for what's right and true, you will receive both hate and love, but everyone will know what you are fighting for. (Unknown)

How many women have been screwed over in sports because we *must* allow a man who wants to be called a woman to enter women's sports because they suck in their own sport as men but can dominate in women's sports? Yeah, that makes so much sense.

Lia (William) Thomas is an absolute disgrace to swimming and Riley Gaines was tragically left in the wake of this idiotic leftist ideology and something must be done. Women have fought for too long to have equal rights and to be able to compete in sports at the highest level equally among natural-born females. It is *common knowledge* that women are not created physically equal to men and would have *no chance* at beating them. *Duh*! Although I will have to point out that Riley Gaines and Lia (William) Thomas tied in their swim meet race. And for whatever incredibly stupid reason that the judges came up with, they still gave the medal to Lia (William). *Wow*, totally *unbelievable*!

So whose feelings are being hurt here? Because of this nonsense, whose dreams are being shot down and made to feel that they don't matter? That *all* their hard work to get to this level of their sport *doesn't matter*? The nonsense just continues.

But as I started this chapter, the ugliness and the destruction of this kind of mental dysphoria is seeping into every crevasse of life and throughout the world. It is taking over our schools, our workplaces, our governments, and even into our churches. Denominations are accepting this and approving and marrying same-sex marriages. What scripture are you reading? What version of the Bible do you have to learn and teach from? Too often and throughout history, mankind wants to cut and paste their own version of God's Word to fit their own sinful ways so they will not feel convicted. You cannot mock God, nor can you change what his Word already says. You can twist anything you want to fit into your box, but God will smash that box, that twisted ideology, to pieces.

Before you start throwing stones, please know and understand, I don't hate these people who are choosing to live their lives in this way. I actually love them, but I disagree with their lifestyle. It goes against the whole family dynamic and how it was originally created to be. You can throw all sorts of facts at me and the history of the gay community, I get it. It has been around for as long as humans have been on the earth. But it still goes against the scriptures and what God calls sin. We don't get to change what is sin and what is not to fit our lifestyle or some new ideology.

> However, as it is written: "No eye has seen,
> no ear has heard, no mind has conceived what

God has prepared for those who love Him—but God has revealed it to us by His Spirit.

"The Spirit searches all things, even the deep things of God. For who among men knows the thoughts of a man except the man's spirit within him? In the same way no one knows the thoughts of God except the Spirit of God. We have not received the spirit of the world but the Spirit who is from God, that we may understand what God has freely given us. This is what we speak, not in words taught us by human wisdom but in words taught by the Spirit, expressing spiritual truths in spiritual words. The man without the Spirit does not accept the things that come from the Spirit of God, for they are foolishness to him, and he cannot understand them, because they are spiritually discerned. The spiritual man makes judgments about all things, but he himself is not subject to any man's judgment.

"For who has known the mind of the Lord that he may instruct Him? But we have the mind of Christ." (Paul, 1 Corinthians 2:9–16)

Jesus says…"Let go of your complaints, forgive those who loved you poorly, step over your feelings of being rejected, and have the courage to trust that you won't fall into an abyss of nothingness but into the safe embrace of a God whose love will heal all your wounds." (Henri Nouwen)

Our biggest hurdle is to continue to fight against that which is a lie, but is believed to be true by many who want to shove their ideologies so far down our throats that we will have to swallow their vicious agenda, which includes the mutilation of children. The blind will stay blind because their hearts are hardened. Those who have been hurt by the world, by church, by religion, by pastors, priests, and clergy, those who have been hurt by the ones that were supposed to love them, how can they feel loved and wanted when all they are feeling is pain, hurt, abuse, and abandonment? The recourse and ripple effect of such pain and confusion has been building for generations and generations. Spilling down on each new generation, the sins of the past being given and handed down to the next set of children.

To try and even add up the countless number of boys and girls, especially boys, over many, many decades who were sexually abused by their very own priests and clergy in the Catholic Church is explicably tragic on too many levels.

Thousands upon thousands upon thousands of boys forever scarred, forever broken, forever changed for the rest of their lives, struggling to understand not only *how* this happened, but why? And even more importantly, "Why God? Why did this have to happen to me?"

The absolute desecration and destruction, the ripple effect that this would cause would end up affecting so many lives, so many marriages, so many other children who would then be pushed into the same twisted sexual abuse from the men who were abused as children. The cycle goes on and on, the rippling circles continuing on, pressing on every side and leaving insurmountable damage in its wake. Crippling the lives of multiple generations.

And we wonder, what is wrong with our world?

This is the repetitive reaction. Hurt people hurt people.

And so from the ashes of years and years of these forms of destruction, we now lie in the stench of this abominable pile of sin that will most likely not be vanquished but will only continue to grow more vile heads of evil with reaching arms and venturing legs of despicable and destructive sin.

The healing that is necessary to turn this around will take hundreds of years, and even then, it may never be the same. But God…

Even in the shadow of our own demise, there is a light that shines ever so brightly. There is the possibility of healing from the pain of this world. There is hope beyond what wants to bring us down. But we need to stand up against the evil of this world and call it what it is. I believe Jesus is trying to wake us up and stand up to be seen and heard. No more timidness, no more hiding or being ashamed of Jesus. God needs soldiers who will put on the armor of God and fight!

> Finally, be strong in the Lord and His mighty power. Put on the full armor of God so that you can take your stand against the devil's schemes. For our struggle is not against flesh and blood, but against the rulers, against the authorities, against the powers of this dark world and against the spiritual forces of evil in the heavenly realms. Therefore, put on the full armor of God, so that when the day of evil comes, you may be able to stand your ground, and after you have done everything, to stand. Stand firm then, with the belt of truth buckled around your waist, with the breastplate of righteousness in place, and with your feet fitted with the readiness that comes from the gospel of peace. In addition to all this, take up the shield of faith, with which you can extinguish all the flaming arrows of the evil one. Take the helmet of salvation and the sword of the Spirit, which is the Word of God. And pray in the Spirit on all occasion with all kinds of prayers and requests. (Paul, Ephesians 6:10–18)

The call to arms is now! The harvest is ripe, and the trumpets will soon be sounding the alarm. The war is not over and the battle for souls continues to get more challenging. God is sending his army; in fact, they have already been dispatched. His command is swift and to the point. We, who truly call Jesus Lord, must obey the call of the Great Commandment.

> Then Jesus came to them and said, "All authority in heaven and on earth has been given to me. Therefore, go and make disciples of all

nations, baptizing them in the name of the Father and of the Son and of the Holy Spirit, and teaching them to obey everything I have commanded you. And surely, I am with you always, to the very end of the age." (Jesus, Matthew 28:18–20)

There is a reason why the Apostle Paul tells us to put on the full armor of God. For we are truly soldiers for Christ, believe this or not. You are either sold out for God or you are not. You are either doing his will or yours.

God called us to Love people. He did not call us to agree with them. Just because someone does not agree with you does not mean they are judging you or hate you. (Unknown)

A sin is a sin. You sin, I sin, we all sin. And Jesus died for *all of that sin*. You either accept his offering of eternal life, freedom from sin, a hope that never ends and the truth that is revealed through the Holy Spirit or you don't.

The world doesn't give peace, for it doesn't have any peace to give. It fights for peace, it negotiates for peace...But Jesus gives peace to those who put their trust in Him. (Billy Graham)

If I were you, I would want to know with concrete evidence that my faith is spot on with Jesus and the scriptures. "Please, Lord, let me be seen righteous in your eyes."

Well done good and faithful servant. Enter into my Father's Kingdom. (Jesus)

This…this is what you should be 100 percent focused on. *Not what the world* sees as right and true, but what *Jesus sees* as right and true. We, as mere humans, do not get to, or have the power to, decide what is right and wrong in the world in which our incredible Creator *created*.

Are you God? Do *you* get to say what is right and wrong? According to the scripture written by Don Baunsgard? *I don't think so.* Not even close, pal! We all need to take our self-righteousness and pride and ego and falsehood and flush it down the toilet because that is what it is…a bunch of crap!

I'm keeping it real, folks, just keeping it real! There is no time for this nonsense. I have no time for this nonsense. We already have *so* much else to keep at bay with all the lies and deceit of our government and our leadership. But if this is where the direction of the earth is heading, so be it. It only confirms with even more accuracy the prophecies that were written close to two thousand years ago.

Maybe, just maybe, we will be lucky enough to be the ones raptured. Oh, how sweet that would be.

> Pride is spiritual cancer. It eats up the very possibility of love or contentment or even common sense. (C. S. Lewis)

> All that is gold does not glitter, not all those who wander are lost; the old that is strong does not wither, deep roots are not reached by the frost. From the ashes a fire shall be woken, a light from the shadows shall spring; renewed shall the blade that was broken, the crownless again shall be king. (J. R. R. Tolkien)

In the very true and profound words of Popeye the Sailorman, "I ams what I ams!"

We've all heard this verse: "So God created man in His own image, in the image of God He created him; male and female he created them" (Genesis 1:27).

Personally, I will stick to the Word of God and trust and believe in this. Anything else is just a fairy tale.

> If the Bible calls it a sin…our opinion doesn't matter. (Unknown)

> When Jesus hung out with sinners…they changed…He didn't. (Unknown)

And lastly and this one is *spot on*:

> Tolerance is the last virtue of a depraved society. When you have an immoral society that has blatantly, proudly, violated all of the commandments of God, there is one last virtue they insist upon: tolerance for their immorality. (D. James Kennedy)

Who am I? I am a son of the King, a child of God. Who are you?

> My aim is to awaken some from the rut. I know it is impossible to awaken everybody, but I hope to awaken some. I use the word awaken here advisedly and carefully because the Bible contains significant teaching gathered around the word sleep. There is…first of all…natural sleep. "He grants sleep to those he loves"—Psalm 127:2. "I will lie down and sleep in peace, for you alone, O Lord, make me dwell in safety"—Psalm 4:8…I am thinking of moral sleep and spiritual sleep. Moral sleep is suggested in First Corinthians 15:34, "Awake to righteousness and sin not" (KJV). There is such a thing as moral sleep. It is entirely possible to be displeasing God and grieving the Holy Spirit by being asleep mor-

ally; that is, by permitting what should not be allowed.

Most people do not want to hear this. They want something added to what they have. They do not want to be told that they are permitting something that should not be allowed. In other words, they are doing what they should not be doing. But you ask, "Is it true of Christians? Do you believe that many Christians are doing this?" I have no hesitation in saying that all the symptoms in the church today point to Christians doing things they should not be doing and failing to do what they should be doing. That is the positive and the negative—the sins of commission, and sins of omission. To be unaware of these sins is to be morally asleep. (A. W. Tozer, *Sermon: Moral Sleep*)

Our culture has accepted two *huge lies*.
The first lie…is that if you disagree with someone's lifestyle,
you must fear or hate them.
The second lie…is that to love someone
means you agree with everything
they believe or do. Both are nonsense.
You don't have to compromise convictions to be compassionate.

—Rick Warren

CHAPTER 7

Predestined

And we know that in all things God works for the good of those who love Him, who have been called according to His purpose. For those God foreknew He also predestined to be conformed to the likeness of His Son, that He might be the firstborn among many brothers. And those He predestined, He also called; those He called, He also justified; those He justified, He also glorified.
—Paul, Romans 8:28–30

The Word of God is the anvil upon which
the opinions of men are smashed.
—Charles Spurgeon

"God works for the good of those who *love him*" (emphasis mine). You just read that in the verse above. I repeated it because of the powerfully deep message that is buried within these ten words.

As I wrote in my last book, the thirty-year orchestrated plan that God had for me that which of course I knew nothing about had been predestined by God.

Why? Simply because I chose to love him. And I chose to love him because he first loved me. I cannot begin to say that I have any idea, the thoughts or plans of God. I just listen, obey, and then move.

Ask anyone who has known me most of my life and they will tell you, never in a lifetime would they have ever dreamed that this guy would write a book or a fourth for that matter. But I believe that God absolutely knew.

God has an innate ability to tap into and refine like gold the gifts and talents that he bestowed upon us for one reason, and that is to use us to fulfill his plan and to glorify him. All we must do is step in faith and trust in him that his plan will unfold just as he intended within his will, not ours. Along the way, we get the chance to become more like his Son and actually see miracles happen, prayers answered, and amazing stories be told.

The whole COVID "plandemic," as I like to call it, opened the eyes of many who didn't see something like this coming down the pike. You can call me a conspiracy theorist all you want; that doesn't bother me in the slightest, but I do believe that this whole COVID ordeal was also a predestined, preplanned event. It was wrapped up in the diabolical plans of the Great Reset which was orchestrated by the World Economic Forum as a "response" to the COVID-19 plandemic. Building momentum behind the curtain in their high places, like the Blackrock Corp, Vanguard, and others, forces have joined with the likes of Bill Gates and George Soros to implement a One World government. This would include a one-world currency. If you look deep enough, you will find that there is already technology out there like the RFID chip that can be implanted under your skin and into the hand with all of your information tracked in that microscopic chip. You can even look up an army psy-ops ad online that spells it all out. These people who have sold their souls for power in this life are fully committed to distracting humanity and controlling everyone for their own worldly gain.

Hmmm, one more step closer to the realization of prophecy foretold almost two thousand years ago.

You don't have to be a rocket scientist to put two and two together to form this mathematical equation. The writing is on the wall. You only have to stop long enough to read it. You only need to put down your cell phone long enough to catch a glimpse that something's not right that is taking place before our very eyes, and they are passing these laws right under our nose. When you start to realize there is an elaborate scheme constructed to keep you distracted, then you start to see the real picture. Like one of those 3D posters we used to stare at in the '90s to see the picture hidden inside. But our distractions are in our hands. We prefer the fantasy of our own virtual reality to the one that exists around us physically, and we prefer to live in physical comfort, so we rarely tend to step outside of it to even help another person. Believe it or not, this has been orchestrated to keep us *away from* God.

I will even take this once step further to proclaim that it is totally possible for God to open the eyes of those who believe *to see clearly* and know deep within by Holy Spirit's nudging, that what is going on around us is in fact the beginnings of a predetermined set of outcomes that *have* to take place so as to fulfill the predestined prophecies that are unfolding before us. And those who are blind to see clearly what is taking place, just as many of us *knew* deep down and from the wisdom provided us by the Holy Spirit that the COVID-19 deal was in fact a ploy to insert into our bodies, unbeknownst to us, predetermined chemicals that would begin the plans to fulfill what the Great Reset was truly all about. And that was to decrease the population of the world among many other secondary goals. Take a look around. Consider how many people you know who have died after taking the experimental vaccine. There are a lot. Now how many do you know who are otherwise healthy and did not take it who have died? Or even observe how many people who took it and have odd new health issues like lung diseases, autoimmune diseases, heart problems, vision problems, recurrence of cancer, and so much more? The experiment backfired, and those who allowed the test to happen on them are paying the price.

And guess what? It worked like a charm. Most people fell for it, and many regret it. The statistics alone are mind-boggling.

When this all first came out in March of 2020, shutting down the entire world for a virus and the concurrent chatter about potential vaccines, my wife, Lena, immediately jumped on the internet to find peer-reviewed medical journal articles around the mRNA technology and what she found out was absolutely crazy. If I can get the story right, the mRNA vaccine that was already produced was not allowed to be used because it could not get approval from the proper authorities, the FDA, and had been turned down time and time again. (Lena's note: As the information about COVID was coming out to us, I was intimately following every conversation. My background is in exercise science, and I have a fairly decent layman's comprehension of cellular level physiology and biological chemistry. I found the conversations fascinating, and I actually enjoy reading peer-reviewed journal articles to the extent that I pay for annual access to them. That said, I would also like to add that back in the '90s when the military was forced to take the experimental anthrax vaccine, I refused and was reprimanded and forced out for it. Congress later deemed their legal position as unconstitutional which allowed me to go back into the military, which I did, and recently retired from. However, the military *did* have to redesign the anthrax vaccine because of the extensive health issues the original formula caused. I was not going to fall for that again, so I stood up with several thousand others and refused the COVID EUA vaccine and was barely able to retire. Finally, of note regarding the mRNA reference Don made, those who were designing it had been trying for thirty years to get CDC approval to run controlled tests on humans, but it was constantly denied because of the danger it imposed due to the role of the mRNA within the cell. The controlled tests, though admittedly often dangerous, are the most logical way to determine the efficacy of a vaccine. That doesn't mean I think this should ever have been authorized. But had it been offered in a controlled setting, with parameters established and managed, accountability for complications honored, and peer-reviewed evaluation, it would have been earlier identified that this was an extremely dangerous product to inject into human bodies. Furthermore, as it has since been revealed, these vaccines that were rushed to production and arbitrarily administered were far from controlled and authorized *without medical accountability*, thereby allowing innocent people to be physiologically damaged or even murdered for the sake of population control and human corralling. Those who pushed them on us knew quite well that it typically takes numerous years to produce a proper vaccine and test it with thorough evaluation for the safety of *all people*, regardless of their individual chemistry, prior to ever even considering it for wide dissemination. True vaccines are never rushed, it's too dangerous. Okay, I'm stepping off my soapbox and moving back to my editorial role now.)

When Lena went back to try and find those peer reviews, they were gone. Completely disappeared. And if you remember, many doctors and nurses, hundreds, if not thousands, were fired because they stood up against this vaccine and made it known that it was *not* a good idea. It was purely an experimental drug that was *not* tested properly, and this is why it was never approved by the FDA.

But yet it was pushed; it was shoved down our throats and into our faces. People lost their jobs, people were cut off from their families, churches were shut down, with example after example of dirty tricks to coerce the people to get the vaccine. The government offering lottery tickets (did anyone get paid?), free food, along with so many other examples of coercion. This alone should have made everyone stop and say, "What the heck?" And it did. My wife and I were adamant about fighting against this world-devised plan to make it mandatory for everyone to have to get the jab.

We were heckled, bullied, made fun of and even had our own family members ridicule us in front of the entire world on social media. Why? For a made-up vaccine that had *proven nothing* to fight COVID-19. What a flippin' joke. And now the truth is out. Yet many still will not listen to the facts; they will only listen to what they want to hear.

> Cures don't kill people.
> Cures don't injure people.
> Cures don't make magnets stick to you.
> Cures don't segregate people.
> Cures don't bribe people.
> Cures don't need liability clauses.
> Cures don't need PR campaigns.
> Cures don't need censorship. (Danny Gokey)

Fear is the factor which brings about the most powerful motivator. For those who don't believe that Jesus is their absolute Savior, fear becomes everything. When you don't believe in God, when you don't believe in heaven or hell, then this life becomes all there is. I do believe though, deep down, the fear that resides in those who choose not to believe, that there will be moments where their conscience gets the best of them and is quietly telling them, "What if it is true? What if there really is a hell?" Then the fear becomes ten times as heavy around their neck as they try with all their might to control the outcome of their current existence. They believe they have the power to control how long they are on this earth. When in reality, nobody can stop the outcome of death taking its toll on each of us. And nobody can predict when and how each of us are going to die. Unless of course, you take it into your own hands and make your death come a lot sooner than planned.

> Wrong is wrong even if everyone is doing it. Right is right even if no one is doing it. (Saint Augustine of Hippo)

This quote I am about to show you was written in 1948, seventy-five years ago, but I believe it is as relevant and spot on for the subject matter we are looking at right now and at a time such as this:

> In one way we think a great deal too much of the atomic bomb. "How are we to live in an atomic age?"
> I am tempted to reply: "Why, as you would have lived in the sixteenth century when the plague visited London almost every year, or as you would have lived in the Viking age when raiders from Scandinavia might land and cut your throat on any given night; or indeed, as you are already living in an age of cancer, an age of syphilis, and age of paralysis, an age of air raids, an age of railway accidents, an age of motor accidents.
> "In other words, do not let us begin by exaggerating the novelty of our situation. Believe

me, dear sir or madam, you and all whom you love were already sentenced to death before the atomic bomb was invented: and quite a high percentage of us were going to die in unpleasant ways. We had, indeed, one very great advantage over our ancestors—anesthetics; but we have that still. It is perfectly ridiculous to go about whimpering and drawing long faces because the scientists have added one more chance of painful and premature death to a world which already bristled with such chances and in which death itself was not a chance at all, but a certainty.

"This is the first point to be made: and the first action to be taken is to pull ourselves together. If we are all going to be destroyed by an atomic bomb, let that bomb when it comes find us doing sensible and human things—praying, working, teaching, reading, listening to music, bathing the children, playing tennis, chatting to our friends over a pint and a game of darts—not huddled together like frightened sheep and thinking about bombs. They may break our bodies (a microbe can do that) but they need not dominate our minds." (C. S. Lewis, 1948)

Well said, sir, very well said.

I will try with as much certainty as I can to sum up what Mr. Lewis is making abundantly obvious. We are all going to die. But we have a choice in how we choose to live out our daily lives. When you allow fear to rule your world, this can cause your life to become crippled with anxiety. And that is *no way* to live. You have been given this one life to live. Live it with great joy, much laughter, good friends, and your loved ones close by. But to live in fear, especially with how much our news outlets, our social media, you name it, has consumed and brainwashed so many inhabitants of this great planet earth. It is sickening to sit back and watch people allow those who do not have the authority over you, to control you, and literally make you believe that death is on your front porch.

Well, unless you do this or take that or jab yourself with something straight into your body that has not been thoroughly tested and has not proven to change anyone's chances of getting Covid or passing it along. It is complete and utter nonsense.

> If you cannot think for yourself, you are not intelligent, period. Not questioning information fed to you through schooling, the government or the media and simply regurgitating it as being true because you have blind faith in those entities is not intelligence, it's obedience. (Unknown)

Do you have any idea, or maybe you do, of how many people I have heard of who got the vaccine who still got Covid-19? And how many have been affected physically by the shot? These are just those I know and have heard of. It is astronomical. But then again, what do I know? I am not a doctor or a scientist. Oh right, they know everything, and they absolutely know what is best for us! What a crock of crap that is! Throw in a bunch of politicians, actors, and professional sports players, all vying to tell you how wrong you are and that you are punk, a schmuck, a danger to society, etc., etc.

I tell you what, I am going to trust in Jesus, and you can trust in whomever you want.

If it is my time, then it is my time. Only God knows when that is.

> For He chose us in Him before the creation of the world to be holy and blameless in His sight. In love He predestined us to be adopted as His sons through Jesus Christ, in accordance with His pleasure and will—to the praise of His glorious grace, which He has freely given us in the One He loves. In Him we have redemption through His blood, the forgiveness of sins, in accordance with the riches of God's grace that

He lavished on us with all wisdom and understanding. And He made known to us the mystery of His will according to His good pleasure, which He purposed in Christ, to be put into effect when the times will have reached their fulfillment—to bring all things in heaven and on earth together under one head, even Christ.

In Him we were also chosen, having been predestined according to the plan of Him who works out everything in conformity with the purpose of His will, in order that we, who were the first to hope in Christ, might be for the praise of His glory. And you were also included in Christ when you heard the word of truth, the gospel of your salvation. Having believed, you were marked in Him with a seal, the promised Holy Spirit, who is a deposit guaranteeing our inheritance until the redemption of those who are God's possession—to the praise of His glory. (Paul, Ephesians 1:4–14)

Hallelujah and Amen!

This confirmation found again and again throughout the Bible is the life blood that produces hope and continually kindles the fire that has been placed within our hearts and souls, the Holy Spirit, which guides us and teaches us, helping us to see things as they really are so that we would know better than to listen to the wisdom of man, which is always filled with evil tongues dripping with some form of poison, looking to devour anyone gullible enough to listen and follow and obey.

The devil is always prowling around in the hearts and souls of men and women who have sold out for the evil of this world instead of seeking out the one who truly loves them more than they will ever know.

Free will.

God will not force you to love him. He will not force you to love his Son, even though he sent him to earth to die for you and me. Free will is love in and of itself. Because the God of the universe and all of creation is saying to you, "I could have chosen to control you and made you do what I want, but that would not produce true love but only false love, fake love, a puppeteer with his barrage of puppets."

> Love is nothing without action. Trust is nothing without proof. Sorry is nothing without change. (Unknown)

God is fully in charge. He knows all too well what is going to happen tomorrow. We, on the other hand, do not.

It might be in your best interest to investigate the subjects I am bringing to the table. My intention from the very beginning is to bring the darkness into the light so that it can be exposed. Please don't misunderstand. I am not claiming that everything I am saying is spot on or even absolutely the truth. But what I won't do is just follow along without questioning it. This is our God-given right. We are allowed to ask questions; we are allowed to doubt, to wonder, to make decisions about our own health care. That is not something that can or should be forced upon us. Just like I would *never* force upon anyone to believe exactly what I believe or to give an ultimatum that someone would have to go against their better judgment and do something that would be against their beliefs.

We *must* be better than that; we must *do* better than that.

> The vague and tenuous hope that God is too kind to punish the ungodly has become a deadly opiate for the consciences of millions. (A. W. Tozer)

There will come a time, though, where the people of this world, all of them that are left, will have no choice but to take the mark of the beast or be tortured and killed. It is a matter of eternal life or eternal death. Hear me now, *loud and clear*, if you find yourself in the future and all the true Christians are gone as well as all the children, then know that the time is near. I tell you now so you will know if you are left behind, *do not take the mark of the beast*. No matter what, let death come to you, but do not allow that mark on your right hand or forehead make its way there. If you do, you are sealed to your doom in the gates of hell for eternity. And there will be weeping and gnashing of teeth and unspeakable horror.

This future event is predestined. Each of our deaths is predestined by God. He holds the time in his hands. Open your eyes and see. Look and ask God to show you so you can know and understand the things that are to come, that which has already happened, and to know the difference.

The Bible, especially the New Testament, is filled with eye-popping wisdom and truth, a love so amazing and a Savior so full of grace and mercy and forgiveness, it is hard to believe sometimes but is absolutely true and genuine. Read it. Read it daily. Read it now. *Know it*. It is absolutely a matter of life or death. Eternal life or eternal death.

Amazing grace, how sweet the sound.

> A lie doesn't become truth, wrong does not become right and evil doesn't become good just because it's accepted by a majority. (Booker T. Washington)

Okay, one more, and this one is good:

> A fact is information minus emotion. An opinion is information plus experience. Ignorance is an opinion lacking information. And stupidity is an opinion that ignores fact. (Unknown)

The time is now. *Now*. Each second that ticks by is one more chance lost. You and I only get so many seconds in this one life. Do you care more about the years of this life, or would it seem more important to think about what comes next?

Eternity. People die every day. Every age group in hundreds of different ways. Death is impalpable and something we don't want to face, but it is inevitable. Truth cannot be swept aside.

In the movie *Star Wars*, which I love by the way, Princess Leia risks her life and many others to capture and redistribute secret plans of the Death Star back to the rebel base through a droid called R2-D2. With these plans, she sends a video message contained in a DVD/CD-like compartment located on R2-D2. As Luke Skywalker is trying to clean the droid, out pops this 3-D video message, which shows Leia pleading for help from someone named Obi-Wan Kenobi. She goes on to explain how she has hidden the secret plans of the Death Star in this droid, then she goes on to plead for help from Obi-Wan.

> General Kenobi. Years ago…you served my father in the clone wars. Now he begs you to help him in the struggle against the Empire. I regret that I am unable to present my father's request to you in person, but my ship has fallen under attack and my mission to bring you to Alderaan has failed. I have placed information vital to the survival of the rebellion into the memory systems of this R2 unit. My father will know how to retrieve it. You must see this droid safely delivered to him on Alderaan. This is our most desperate hour. Help me, Obi-Wan Kenobi…You're our only hope.

I have thought of this scene many, many times throughout my life, redirecting that last sentence to Jesus and inserting his name instead of Obi-Wan Kenobi.

> This is our most desperate hour. Help us, Lord Jesus. You're our only hope.

SURRENDER

To me, and I would assume many others, this is how we see our world in such a desperate time as this. Jesus is our only hope. And I do pray every day, "Help us, Lord Jesus…help us."

He is our only hope.

> Abiding in Christ means allowing His Word to fill our minds, direct our wills, and transform our affections. (Sinclair B. Ferguson)

> The measure of a life, after all, is not its duration, but its donation. (Corrie Ten Boom)

> First we overlook evil. Then we permit evil. Then we legalize evil. Then we promote evil. Then we celebrate evil. Then we persecute those who still call it evil.
>
> Woe unto them who call evil, good, and good, evil! (Isaiah 5:20)

THE SURRENDERING

Jesus said, "I have chosen you. I have called you by name." Every day you have to say, "Yes." Total surrender. To be where He wants you to be. If He puts you in the street, if everything is taken from you and suddenly you find yourself in the street, to accept to be in the street at that moment. Not for you to put yourself in the street. But to accept to be there. This is quite different. To accept if God wants you to be in a palace, alright, to accept to be in the palace, as long as you are not choosing to be in the palace. This is the difference in total surrender. To accept whatever He gives. And to give whatever it takes, with a big smile. This is the surrender to God. To accept to be cut to pieces and yet every piece belongs only to Him. This is the surrender. To accept all the people that come, the work that you happen to do. Today maybe you have a good meal and tomorrow maybe you have nothing. There is no water in the pump. All right, to accept. And to give whatever it takes. It takes your good name, it takes your health, it takes… Yes, That is the Surrender. You are free then.

—Mother Teresa

CHAPTER 8

Heart of Stone

People have asked me if our present generation would gladly accept Jesus if He came at this time, instead of 2,000 years ago. I have to believe that history does repeat itself! In our own day, many who want to follow the Christian traditions still balk and reject a thorough—going spiritual housecleaning within their own lives. When Jesus came, many realized that it would mean probable financial loss for them to step out and follow Christ. Also, many of those men and women who considered the claims of Christ in His day knew that following Him would call for abrupt and drastic changes in their patterns of living. The proud and selfish aspects of their lives would have been disturbed. Beyond that, there was almost a complete disdain for the inward spiritual life which Jesus taught as a necessity for mankind; that it is the pure in heart who will see God! I am afraid that humanity's choice would still be the same today. People are still more in love with money and pride and pleasure than they are with God and His salvation!
—A.W. Tozer, Sermon: If Jesus Came Today

We are not saved by obedience, for obedience is the result of salvation. We are saved by faith because faith leads us to obey.
—Charles Spurgeon

> There was this one time someone said to me…"I don't
> believe in God because there is so much suffering in
> the world. That's how I know God doesn't exist."
> And I go…"Well, okay, If God doesn't exist…
> is there still suffering in the world?"
> And they go…"Well, yes."
> I said, "Then who is responsible now?"
> "Well, we are."
> I said, "Now, if were responsible for the suffering,
> and there is no God, is it possible there is a God…
> and He is really upset that we have allowed so much
> suffering? That this is beneath our intention?"
> Human beings are the only species that can live beneath
> their intention. You will never see a beaver create a
> bridge. It will only create a dam. Silkworms will only
> create silk. Never polyester. Humans are the only
> species that can actually subvert their intention.
>
> —Sean Busby

The depths of a man's soul are only as deep as he allows himself to see it. Either you know it is there or you are oblivious to it. Many who live do not live to gratify the soul but to gratify the flesh. We choose to only see what we want to see, hear only what we want to hear.

Our objective and our main purpose in this life has either been created through the experiences of the flesh or through the transformation of the heart and soul through supernatural, spiritual contact with the Savior. It may seem to be true, and I am no scholar, but I believe that God makes it clear through his Word that he hardens the hearts of whom he chooses and has mercy on whom he wants to have mercy.

I have to stop and wonder and say to myself, "Self, it might behoove you to investigate why some people seriously choose to not know Jesus while others seek him out diligently. Why is this?" And throughout my studies of scripture, I have found it to be clear that this is in fact what is happening. Let me read to you this scripture out of Romans.

> It is not as though God's Word had failed. For not all who are descended from Israel are Israel. Nor because they are his descendants are they all Abraham's children. On the contrary, it is through Isaac that your offspring will be reckoned. In other words, it is not the natural children who are God's children, but it is the children of the promise who are regarded as Abraham's offspring. For this was how the promise was stated: "At the appointed time I will return, and Sarah will have a son."
>
> Not only that, but Rebekah's children had one and the same father, our father, Isaac. Yet, before the twins were born or had done anything good or bad—In order that God's purpose in election might stand: not by works but by him who calls—she was told, "The older will serve the younger." Just as it is written: "Jacob I loved, but Esau I hated."
>
> What then shall we say? Is God unjust? Not at all! For He says to Moses, "I will have mercy on whom I have mercy, and I will have compassion on whom I have compassion."
>
> It does not, therefore, depend on man's desire or effort, but on God's mercy. For the Scripture says to Pharoah: "I raised you up for this very purpose, that I might display my power in you and that my name might be proclaimed in all the earth." Therefore, God has mercy on whom He wants to have mercy, and He hardens whom He wants to harden.
>
> One of you will say to me: "Then why does God still blame us? For who resists His will?" But

> who are you, O man, to talk back to God? Shall what is formed say to Him who formed it, "Why did you make me like this?" Does not the potter have the right to make out of the same lump of clay some pottery for noble purposes and some for common use?
>
> What if God, choosing to show His wrath and make His power known, bore with great patience the objects of His wrath—prepared for destruction? What if He did this to make the riches of His glory known to the objects of His mercy, whom He prepared in advance for glory—even us, whom He also called, not only from the Jews but also from the Gentiles? (Paul, Romans 9:6–24)

It is not far from the imagination or even to underestimate the possibility that God has already preordained those whom he chooses to fulfill his purpose. Which would entail both the objects of his mercy and the objects in which he chooses to harden their hearts. Both, ultimately, will produce the results needed to fulfill God's predestined plan, which is always in full swing. Whether we choose to believe it or not.

As I have scoured the landscape of this planet earth over the course of my fifty-four years, seeking a deeper understanding of the complexities of man, it has been easily bogged down by the trappings of a heart so dark to want to turn away from the atrocities that seem so easily willed from one man to the next. I am stunned at such cruelty, shocked at the level of hatred poured out viciously on every man, woman, and child. We see it every day, read about it from all over the world in our newspapers, our media, and in our textbooks.

Yet time seems to bring no relief, no change in the hearts of men. Just a repetitive repeat of mass hysteria and destruction dripping with the lust for blood. Just recently, in our time in history, the Palestinians from the Hamas group broke through the border into Israel and slaughtered men, women, and children in cowardly, brutal,

SURRENDER

and barbaric evil ways—1,300 plus dead. All because they have come to believe that this is their command, this is their purpose, and that Jews must be murdered according to their radical Muslim religion.

Sadly, this is nothing new to the thousands upon thousands of books throughout history, proclaiming again and again that these atrocities, these wars and the mass murder and death must happen to complete their mission. To complete the purpose in which they were created. War, jealousy, religion, greed, ego, and pride have slaughtered billions over the existence of mankind. You have to wonder, why? Isn't there already enough pain in this world to fill the ocean that we feel the need to manufacture more chaos, more death, more pain, more loss, more wars?

Hardened hearts. It is inevitable that billions upon billions will never step into heaven. Never choose to love with the heart of Jesus. Never forgive with the heart of Christ. Never humble themselves to love their neighbor as they love themselves. But even in the darkness and hardness of men shines a light so bright that they cannot and will not be able to hide from it.

> The heavens receded like a scroll being rolled up, and every mountain and island was removed from its place. Then the kings of the earth, the princes, the generals, the rich, the mighty, and everyone else, both slave and free, hid in caves and among the rocks of the mountains. They called to the mountains and the rocks, "Fall on us and hide us from the face of Him who sits on the throne and from the wrath of the Lamb! For the great day of their wrath has come, and who can withstand it?" (Revelation 6:14–17)

> Let us search ourselves this morning and make our calling and election sure, so that the coming of the Lord may cause no dark forebodings in our mind. O for grace to cast away all hypocrisy, and to be found in Him sincere and

without rebuke in the day of His appearing. (C. H. Spurgeon)

It is all I can do but to lift up my eyes to heaven in absolute belief that not only is God in control, but that his wrath will make all things right. And that the hope that is within will sustain me through the most painful truths that have either already taken place or to that which is to come. God will right all the wrongs and the injustices of this world from the hardness and evil of men; they will be judged, and God's justice will prevail.

As the seasons change, it is no small reminder to see that things must die for them to be reborn again. As Jesus made it very clear in his sermons and his teachings: to live, we must die.

> Now there was a man of the Pharisees named Nicodemus, a member of the Jewish ruling council. He came to Jesus at night and said, "Rabbi, we know you are a teacher who has come from God. For no one could perform the miracles you are doing if God were not with Him."
>
> In reply Jesus declared, "I tell you the truth, no one can see the Kingdom of God unless He is born again."
>
> "How can a man be born when he is old?" Nicodemus asked. "Surely he cannot enter a second time into his mother's womb to be born!"
>
> Jesus answered, "I tell you the truth, no one can enter the kingdom of God unless he is born of water and the Spirit. Flesh gives birth to flesh, but the Spirit gives birth to spirit. You should not be surprised at my saying, 'You must be born again.' The wind blows wherever it pleases. You hear its sound, but you cannot tell where it comes from or where it is going. So, it is with everyone born of the Spirit."
>
> "How can this be?" Nicodemus asked.

"You are Israel's teacher," said Jesus, "And do you not understand these things? I tell you the truth, we speak of what we know, and we testify to what we have seen, but still you people do not accept our testimony. I have spoken to you of earthly things and you do not believe; how then will you believe if I speak of heavenly things? No one has ever gone into heaven except the one who came from heaven—the Son of Man. Just as Moses lifted up the snake in the desert, *so the Son of Man must be lifted up,* that everyone who believes in Him may have eternal life.

"For God so loved the world that He gave His one and only Son, that whoever believes in Him shall not perish but have eternal life. For God did not send His Son into the world to condemn the world, but to save the world through Him. Whoever believes in Him is not condemned, but whoever does not believe stands condemned already because He has not believed in the name of God's one and only Son.

"This is the verdict: Light has come into the world, but men loved darkness instead of light because their deeds were evil. Everyone who does evil hates the light and will not come into the light for fear that his deeds will be exposed. But whoever lives by the truth comes into the light, so that it may be seen plainly that what He has done has been done through God." (Jesus, John 3:1–21 [emphasis mine])

The scriptures are extravagant. They are lush with wisdom, truth, and love, and they leave you standing there with your jaw slightly ajar with a look of shock and awe as you try and breathe in the depths of its meaning.

And yet so, so, many choose not to listen. Choose not to see so clearly the treasure right in front of them. Choose to not accept the free gift of salvation. Choose to not acknowledge who should be the Lord of their lives. Choose to not invest in the research of the most important subject in the history of all of mankind. Choose not to understand and realize the importance of the soul and where it may be going. So many choose not to repent and allow their heart to remain stone.

> Supposing there was no intelligence behind the universe, no creative mind. In that case, nobody designed my brain for the purpose of thinking. It is merely that when the atoms inside my skull happen, for physical or chemical reasons, to arrange themselves in a certain way, this gives me, as a by-product, the sensation I call thought. But, if so, how can I trust my own thinking to be true? It's like upsetting a milk jug and hoping that the way it splashes itself will give you a map of London. But if I can't trust my own thinking, of course I can't trust the arguments leading to Atheism, and therefore have no reason to be an Atheist, or anything else. Unless I believe in God, I cannot believe in thought: so, I can never use thought to disbelieve in God. (C. S. Lewis)

One of the most influential women of the last one hundred years is Mother Teresa. Her example of a Christ-centered life which was lived out clearly as a daughter of the King is to be commended and, if possible, repeated by as many of us as possible who are called. She truly got it. And she stored up a ton of treasures in heaven. I love what she wrote, and it had to be put into this book:

> People are often unreasonable and self-centered, *Forgive Them Anyway.*

SURRENDER

> If you are kind, people may accuse you of ulterior motives, *Be Kind Anyway.*
>
> If you are honest, people may cheat you, *Be Honest Anyway.*
>
> If you find happiness, people may be jealous, *Be Happy Anyway.*
>
> The good you do today may be forgotten tomorrow, *Do Good Anyway.*
>
> Give the world the best you have, and it may never be enough, *Give Your Best Anyway.*
>
> For you see, in the end, it is between you and God. It was never between you and them anyway. (Mother Teresa)

It is between you and God! Period.

When this time is done, and it will be done, you, me, and every other Joe and Joleen, we will *all* have to stand before God, stand before Jesus, and be held accountable for everything. Either you will be as white as snow because of your relationship with Jesus as your mighty counselor, or he will say to his Father, "I don't know him" or "I don't know her."

This is reality. You don't get to choose which one of your many acts of being good or how generally kind you are to be selected as the keys to the gates of heaven. *The only key is Jesus.* When you deny this key, you are given another one, and you don't want that key.

> See to it brothers, that none of you has a sinful, unbelieving heart that turns away from the living God. But encourage one another daily, as long as it is called Today, so that none of you may be hardened by sin's deceitfulness. We have come to share in Christ if we hold firmly till the end the confidence we had at first. (Hebrews 3:12–14)

Let me ask you a question: if you could see beyond this life, the truth of what comes after this life, which by the way is over in like a blip of time, would you live your life differently? If you knew without a doubt that there is a heaven and a hell, that Jesus is alive and real and Satan wants you in hell and currently, hell is your destination, wouldn't you want to do everything in your power to change that? Wouldn't that become the number 1 *thing* in your life to live for? Change for? Give up everything for?

Satan's greatest tool, or at least one of them, is to repeatedly remind you of who you once were or are currently. What we so easily forget, for those of us who have been forgiven is, you are a new creation. You are no longer a child of the world. Satan no longer has anything to hold over you! You are a son or daughter of the King! You are free! You are forgiven!

A good friend of mine and pastor, Baly Botten, had a captivating sermon that really hit it out of the ballpark. Here is a smidge of that sermon:

> What sort of names do you speak over yourself? What sort of names have others spoken over your life? Maybe think of some title an enemy has given you through a difficult season or some place of deep shame that you've grown from. Maybe it's "unloved," or "failure," or "difficult," "problem," "burden," "not enough," "addict," "broken," "damaged goods," "failed father," "criminal."
>
> Whatever it is, Jesus says, "I call you by a new name and that's not who you will be. I give you a new name as 'Beloved,' as 'Chosen,' as 'Adopted,' as 'Redeemed,' as 'Restored.' That is your new name. And that's what I am going to call you immediately." (Baly Botten)

Life, people, friends, girlfriends, boyfriends, coworkers, parents, neighbors, husbands, wives, and even your own children will hurt you with the names that will either be true or not according to your character and the fruit you produce in your life, the way you act and react.

> They will know you by your fruit. Beware of false prophets who come disguised as harmless sheep but are really vicious wolves. You can identify them by their fruit, that is, by the way they act. Can you pick grapes from thornbushes, or figs from thistles? A good tree produces good fruit, and a bad tree produces bad fruit. A good tree can't produce bad fruit, and a bad tree can't produce good fruit. So every tree that does not produce good fruit is chopped down and thrown into the fire. Yes, just as you can identify a tree by its fruit, so you can identify people by their actions. (Jesus, Matthew 7:15–20)

Many times, throughout the gospels, Jesus interacts with people in their most desperate hour or at a place which transcends time and changes that person in the moment, immediately after meeting Jesus. One of those times was when Jesus purposefully met the woman at the well. This woman had no idea how much her life was going to change after this encounter with the Messiah. By the way, if you have not checked out *The Chosen*, this is a must-see show. *My wife and I absolutely love this show*! The director of *The Chosen*, Dallas Jenkins, nailed this scene, and I was crying many tears as I watched it unfold on the TV screen.

> Now He had to go through Samaria. So He came to a town in Samaria called Sychar, near the plot of ground Jacob had given to his son Joseph. Jacob's well was there, and Jesus, tired as He was from the journey, sat down by the well. It was about the sixth hour.

When a Samaritan woman came to draw water, Jesus said to her, "Will you give me a drink?" (His disciples had gone into town to buy food.)

"The Samaritan woman said to Him, "You are a Jew and I am a Samaritan woman. How can you ask me for a drink?" (For Jews do not associate with Samaritans.)

Jesus answered her, "If you knew the gift of God and who it is that asks you for a drink, you would have asked Him and He would have given you living water."

"Sir," the woman said, "You have nothing to draw with and the well is deep. Where can you get this living water? Are you greater than our father Jacob, who gave us the well and drank from it himself, as did also his sons and his flocks and herds?"

Jesus answered, "Everyone who drinks this water will be thirsty again, but whoever drinks the water I give him will never thirst. Indeed, the water I give him will become in him a spring of water welling up to eternal life."

The woman said to him, "Sir, give me this water so that I won't get thirsty and have to keep coming here to draw water."

He told her, "Go, call your husband and come back."

"I have no husband," She replied.

Jesus said to her, "You are right when you say you have no husband. The fact is, you have had five husbands, and the man you now have is not your husband. What you have just said is quite true."

"Sir," the woman said, "I can see that you are a prophet. Our fathers worshiped on this mountain, but you Jews claim that the place where we must worship is in Jerusalem."

Jesus declared, "Believe me, woman, a time is coming when you will worship the Father neither on this mountain nor in Jerusalem. You Samaritans worship what you do not know, we worship what we do know, for salvation is from the Jews. Yet a time is coming and has now come when the true worshipers will worship the Father in spirit and truth, for they are the kind of worshipers the Father seeks. God is spirit, and his worshipers must worship in spirit and in truth."

The woman said, "I know that Messiah (called Christ) is coming. When He comes, He will explain everything to us."

Then Jesus declared, "I who speak to you am He."

Just then his disciples returned and were surprised to find Him talking with a woman. But no one asked, "What do you want?" or "Why are you talking with her?"

Then, leaving her water jar, the woman went back to the town and said to the people, "Come, see the man who told me everything I ever did. Could this be the Christ?" They came out of the town and made their way toward Him. (John 4:4–30)

This is one of many stories where Jesus impacts someone simply by revealing who he truly is and his love is for everyone. Even a Samaritan woman who already had two strikes against her: one being a woman and the other a Samaritan. Jews and Samaritans hated each other with a passion in the time of Jesus. So this interaction was a huge surprise to this woman and Jesus made himself known to her. He revealed to her that he was the Christ, and she was so excited by the news; she left her water jugs and ran back to town to tell everyone who she met.

Many of us would love to have an encounter such as this. A tangible moment of supernatural surprise suddenly seeing Jesus standing in front us and having a conversation with him. It quite literally could change your whole life. but what if it didn't? That is a scary thought to even imagine.

But thousands upon thousands of Jews did just that. Even after seeing miracle after miracle, the Jews still wanted him dead.

It seems crazy to me to try and even imagine what it must have been like at this time in our history. Here is Jesus, standing before them; after waiting for four hundred years, the Jews have their prophesied Messiah, and now they want to kill him for proclaiming that he is the Christ. What crazy times that must have been. Even crazier still is that this killing of Jesus was also prophesied and had to be fulfilled so that the purpose of his death and resurrection could catapult the rest of humanity into the possibility of eternal life. God knew there was no other way to bridge the gap between himself and his creation.

God wiped out his creation once, excluding only Noah and his family, and he will do it again at the end of days. Meanwhile, his Son had some work to do. He needed to save the world from eternal damnation.

In the grand scheme of things, all of our stories here on earth come to end. Our days are numbered when we are born. Some don't even make it out of the womb before they breathe their first breath. We all hear of the horrors of abortion, but do we ever think twice about it? Not really; some condone it as a necessary evil. I proclaim it as murder. And as the world turns, the drama of our unnecessary evils continue to become declared as good just so we can feel better about ourselves instead of allowing this and so many other sins to convict our hearts to turn away from what is killing us spiritually and crying out to our Savior once more, "Please save us, Lord! Have mercy on me, a sinner."

> Every human embryologist in the world knows that the life of a new individual human being begins at fertilization. It is not a belief. It

> is a scientific fact. (Ward Kischer, PhD, Human Embryologist)

Until we stop, and I mean stop, in our tracks and listen and see, the reality of our world, the corruption, the greed, the sexual dysfunction, and disturbed dysphoria that we have slowly created over decades of sex, drugs, and rock 'n' roll, until we truly set our eyes and our hearts on the decrepit and disgusting world we have created, our hearts will continue to beat and flow with sand, with rock, with cement, not blood, for they are truly hearts of stone, not of flesh. They are in the world and not with Jesus.

My all-time favorite comedian, Timothy Hawkins, was doing a skit about being a rock star and how he always wanted to be one. But as a comedian, he can't just say the beginning of a joke and the audience can finish it like a rock star does. He quotes Bon Jovi singing the song "Livin' on a Prayer," "Oh...we're halfway there..." and then lets the audience finish the rest, "Oh...livin' on a prayer." Then in fun, Tim Hawkins says to the audience, which by the way is filled with mostly Christians, "Oh sure, you haven't read your Bible in a month, but you know every word to 'Livin' on a Prayer'!" which the audience laughs at and simultaneously gasps in their moaning of basically being called out on the truth.

Tim Hawkins, making fun of something sad but true, pulls out all the stops and does a great job of being brutally honest about how true it actually is of those who proclaim to follow Christ but are failing miserably in their walk and relationship with Jesus. This is not something that should be done half-heartedly. God does not want lukewarm followers with stone hearts.

Let me put this in a different light: Jesus did *nothing* for you or me *half-heartedly*. He went all-in for you and me. He gave up everything for us. To the depths of hell and back and through the worst form of torture you could ever imagine. When we don't even try and grasp, even for a minute, what he went through for us, that is a slap to the face. You might as well have been a pharisee. And trust me, there will be many, many who will think they are righteous, but Jesus never knew them.

There will come a moment, in the blink of an eye, when the righteous meet Jesus in the air and the world is void of believers and children, maybe then, people will stop and look and listen, but it will be too late. They will be left behind, clutching their hearts of stone. And there will be wailing and mourning and the weeping and gnashing of teeth.

I recently posted on Facebook, which I do pretty regularly, the truth of who Christ is and what is expected of us (I recognize the fact that what I am sharing with the world, mainly hundreds of friends and acquaintances, with whom many are not believers, may not make sense to them). I proclaim it not with fear tactics but from a place of pure love, for I wish none to perish in hell for eternity. I love them all; even perfect strangers, I love them too! It comes from a swollen heart filled compassionately with love. I am trying to give them the greatest gift of all.

Eternity with Jesus, eternal life.

But many have willed it a no-go possibility. Nothing I say will change that. Their hearts are set in stone. Jesus can change that if they just choose to give him a chance. I am offering the seed. I have made my case for Christ as clear and present as I can. I have done my job wholeheartedly and willingly obeying the Master. The rest is up to him. If you want your heart to be softened to Christ, just ask him. Seek him every day. Serve him with your whole heart and be dedicated to his will.

I know one day, I will get to hear him say, *"Well done, my son, well done."*

> Just because I post a lot of spiritual messages doesn't mean I think I am holier than thou. I fight temptation. It's a battle every day. I need Jesus every day, every hour, every minute, and every second. Thank you, Lord, for not giving up on a sinner like me. (Unknown)

SURRENDER

Repentance is a characteristic of the whole life, not the action of a single moment. (Sinclair Ferguson)

But avoid foolish controversies and genealogies and arguments and quarrels about the law, because these are unprofitable and useless. Warn a divisive person once, and then warn him a second time. After that, have nothing to do with him. You may be sure that such a man is warped and sinful; he is self-condemned. (Paul, Titus 3:9–11)

Biblical warning:

>Sugarcoating preaching is dangerous to your soul. (2 Timothy 4:3–4)

>It is better to *speak the truth* that *hurts* and then *heals*, than *falsehood* that *comforts* and then *kills*. (Author unknown)

CHAPTER 9

Chosen

> So too, at the present time there is a remnant chosen by grace. And if by grace, then it is no longer by works; if it were, grace would no longer be grace.
> —Paul, Romans 11:5

> "Now, this is what the Lord says—He who created you, O Jacob, He who formed you, O Israel: Fear not, for I have redeemed you; I have summoned you by name; you…are mine.
> —Isaiah 43:1 (emphasis mine)

As children, we soon find out how important it is to be chosen from your friends and peers to be on this team or that club. It feels pretty dang good if you got chosen in the first three rounds as each team is selecting their teammates, unless of course, there was only three rounds, then you would have been chosen last.

Cho*sen /CHozn/, adjective: having been selected as the best or most appropriate.

> Brothers, think of what you were when you were called. Not many of you were wise by human standards; not many were influential; not many were of noble birth.

> But God chose the foolish things of the world to shame the wise; God chose the weak things of the world to shame the strong. He chose the lowly things of this world and the despised things—and the things that are not—to nullify the things that are, so that no one may boast before Him. It is because of Him that you are in Christ Jesus, who has become for us wisdom from God—that is, our righteousness, holiness, and redemption. Therefore, as it is written: "Let him who boasts boast in the Lord." (Paul, 1 Corinthians 1:26–31)

Humble, kind of heart, generous, loving, caring, considerate, thoughtful, sincere, friendly, compassionate, now stop for a moment and insert foolish, weak, lowly, and despised. These are the things that God can use in us to change the world and, in the end, make sure to not take any credit but boast of our God who has given us eternal life. The wisdom of God transforms the heart of men and women, and through that transformation, the change happens, and we become righteous in the eyes of Christ. Holy and redeemed.

To be chosen is an honor. To be called out of the ranks and sent into the field to fight, not with sword and shield, not with spear and club, but with love, with the Word of God, and faith.

Many before us throughout history have also been chosen. And many of them have left such a mark that their moment here on earth still reverberates and their ripple effect is still making waves throughout the world in their pursuit to serve the King. Harriet Tubman, William Wilberforce, John Wesley, Billy Graham, Dwight L. Moody, Justin Martyr, Oswald Chambers, Teresa of Avila, Dietrich Bonhoeffer, Ignatius of Antioch, Hudson Taylor, St. Francis of Assisi, John Wycliffe, Soren Kierkegaard, C. S. Lewis, Dorothy Sayers, Fyodor Dostoyevsky, G. K. Chesterton, Harriet Beecher Stowe, John Bunyan, Charles Spurgeon, John Calvin, and Martin Luther…just to name a few.

And how can we forget the original twelve? Simon (whom Jesus named Peter), his brother Andrew, James and John, Philip, Bartholomew, Matthew, Thomas, James, son of Alphaeus, Simon the Zealot, Judas, son of James, and Judas Iscariot, who betrayed Jesus. And don't forget the incredible story of Saul who became Paul.

All chosen by Jesus. Only one of them was chosen for a different purpose. Judas Iscariot. He was chosen, but not for salvation. Judas was chosen as the one who would fulfill the plan of God that was prophesied in the Old Testament in Zechariah 11:12–13. He was chosen to fulfill that prophecy and end the life of Christ by betraying him for thirty pieces of silver. Of course, we all know how the story ends. Jesus died, yes, but came back to life and beat death so we can be with him eternally. Unfortunately, Judas will miss out on eternity for his actions.

Judas was predestined to fulfill the greatest betrayal in history. "Then Satan entered Judas, called Iscariot, one of the Twelve. And Judas went to the chief priests and the officers of the temple guard and discussed with them how he might betray Jesus" (Luke 22:3–4).

Of course, after this major blunder, Judas hung himself instead of seeking forgiveness.

God's plan and his purposes are worked out even in the worst possible events.

> He healed the one who arrested Him, served the one who betrayed Him, and loved the world who crucified Him. That's my Jesus. (Faithster)

> In Him we were also chosen, having been predestined according to the plan of Him who works out everything in conformity with the purpose of His will, in order that we, who were the first to hope in Christ, might be for the praise of His glory. And you also were included in Christ when you heard the word of truth, the gospel of your salvation. Having believed, you were marked in Him with a seal, the promised

> Holy Spirit, who is a deposit guaranteeing our inheritance until the redemption of those who are God's possession—to the praise of His glory. (Paul, Ephesians 1:11–14)

God's purpose is to offer salvation to the world, just as he planned to do long ago. God is sovereign; he is in charge. When your life seems chaotic, rest in this truth: Jesus is Lord, and God is in control. God's purpose to save you cannot be thwarted, no matter what evil Satan tries to pull out of his bag of tricks.

> If you think you've blown God's plan for your life, rest in this… You, my beautiful friend, are not that powerful. (@imteairataylor)

That's the beauty of it all. God already knows who will seek him out and who will not. God already knows who will truly have a transformation of the heart and who will be a hypocrite. To be chosen, you must choose a different life. You must choose to accept that this life is no longer yours and be willing to obey the commandments of God. Is it work? Yes. But his grace is greater. His blessings are more abundant than you can imagine. He has the stamina, the power, the fortitude to *carry you* through any fire. He is God! When you are absolutely 100 percent willing to *no-kidding surrender*, he will pick you up and celebrate you.

> Not everyone who says to me, "Lord, Lord, will enter the kingdom of heaven, but only he who does the will of my Father who is in heaven." (Jesus, Matthew 7:21)

Choice…choose…chosen.

We will all fail. This we must accept. But this is where we get to choose, not only to repent, but pray and ask God to give us strength to overcome our weaknesses, our addictions, and our sin. He will never leave you or forsake you. Once you have genuinely entered into a relationship with Jesus, your will, your choice, then he enters into a relationship with you. God's will, his choice.

You are redeemed. You are a new creation. You are a child of God, and you have been chosen out of a lineup, and you were not chosen last.

> Who shall separate us from the love of Christ? Shall trouble or hardship or persecution or famine or nakedness or danger or sword? As it is written: For your sake we face death all day long; we are considered as sheep to be slaughtered. No, in all these things we are more than conquerors through Him who loved us. For I am convinced that neither death nor life, neither angels nor demons, neither the present nor the future, nor any powers, neither height or depth, nor anything else in all creation, will be able to separate us from the love of God that is in Christ Jesus our Lord. (Paul, Romans 8:35–39)

I would even go so far to say, we are *all* chosen. It is up to us to decide if we *want* to be chosen or not.

> Each of us is an Innkeeper who decides if there is room for Jesus. (Unknown)

Those Who Serve

God has a special place for each of us to serve,
and you have chosen to follow His path.
You have been the *hands*, the *feet*, the *voice*, and the
love of God expressed in many different ways.
You have chosen to honor Him as you have served in His name.

> Thank you for your willingness to give of yourself,
> and be used where God has placed you.
> You have blessed many lives.
> —Unknown

What I just quoted above hangs framed in our store as a reminder of our sacrifice to serve others as the hands and feet of Jesus. He chose us, and so we are then blessed to choose to make a difference in the lives of others with his love, his grace, his mercy.

> Inasmuch as you have done it unto one of the least of these... you did unto Me. (Jesus, Matthew 25:40)

To those who see living a life for Christ as boring, as uneventful, as a chore or too many rules, you are missing the entire point of living out your life to fulfill the *very purpose* for which you were created. You, me, everyone is born to fulfill a purpose. We are called to a higher calling. But if you decide that you aren't worthy or that God doesn't love you, you are gravely mistaken.

> A Christian is not someone who never does wrong, but one who is enabled to repent and pick himself up and begin again, because the Christ-life is inside him. (C. S. Lewis)

One of the things I love to see is when people who are famous come to the reality that none of what they have—their money, fame, cars, popularity, possessions—will bring them joy, true joy. But when they find Jesus, truly find Jesus, then *bam*, they see the light, and a lot of them, not all of them, come to a "meet Jesus moment," and there begins the change, the transformation.

Each of us can be ignorant or stagnant or complacent or a serious procrastinator, a hypocrite, but to face Jesus, none of those will matter. When, not if, you stand before Jesus and he asks you, "How come you have chosen to throw it all away? I chose you and you rebuked me. I called for you, and you refused to listen. I reached out for you, and you ignored my help. I gave you every chance to repent and you procrastinated and believed 'that you had a lot more time,' but now, time has run out. What then shall I do with you?"

When will you understand that time is the most valuable thing and the bank of time is running out of money? I highly recommend that you do whatever it takes to not end up bankrupt of time and have nothing to show for it but the things of this world that will matter not when everything that does matter is your very soul.

> So do not be afraid of them. There is nothing concealed that will not be disclosed or hidden that will not be made known. What I tell you in the dark, speak in the daylight; what is whispered in your ear, proclaim from the roofs. Do not be afraid of those who kill the body but cannot kill the soul. Rather, be afraid of the One who can destroy both soul and body in hell. (Jesus, Matthew 10:26–28)

I don't know about you, but the thought of being in a place of absolute torment with weeping, wailing, and gnashing of teeth for eternity doesn't sit well with me. Why would anyone who knows of this information not be face down on the ground, grieving and mourning the sin they have done and not pleading with Jesus for mercy right now because later will be too late? *Now*!

My heart hurts when I have failed the Lord of my soul to the point of knowing that my sin had a part in hammering in those nine-inch nails into his flesh. Yes, I am redeemed, but this does not mean we should become unaware of the continuation of the sin that will be tempting us for the rest of our lives while here on planet earth.

Forgiveness of sins is not like a vending machine where you can throw a quarter in and ask for forgiveness. Or wait for a month and then shove in five dollars' worth of quarters and say your Hail Mary's and believe that this is enough. Trust me when I say this, God knows your heart! Every inch of it. Do not believe that you can mock God in his gift of mercy to you. Hypocrisy will be dealt with swiftly when that time comes. Jesus touches base on this subject many times with a hint of piss and vinegar because this is something that Jesus hates very much.

Here are just a few:

> He replied, "Isaiah was right when he prophesied about you hypocrites; as it is written: These people honor me with their lips, but their hearts are far from me." (Jesus, Mark 7:6–7)

> They claim to know God, but by their actions they deny Him. They are detestable, disobedient and unfit for doing anything good. (Paul, Titus 1:16)

> Live as free people, but do not use your freedom as a cover-up for evil; live as God's slaves. (1 Peter 2:16)

> Why do you call me "Lord, Lord," and do not do what I say? (Jesus, Luke 6:46)

> Beware of the Teachers of the Law. They like to walk around in flowing robes and love to be greeted with respect in the marketplaces and have the most important seats in the synagogues and the places of honor at banquets. They devour widows' houses and for a show make lengthy prayers. These men will be punished most severely. (Jesus, Luke 20:46–47)

> Do not merely listen to the Word, and so deceive yourselves. Do what it says. Anyone who listens to the Word but does not do what it says is like someone who looks at his face in the mir-

ror and, after looking at himself, goes away and immediately forgets what he looks like. But whoever looks intently into the perfect law that gives freedom and continues in it—not forgetting what they have heard, but doing it—they will be blessed in what they do. (James 1:22–25)

Woe to you, teachers of the law and Pharisees, you hypocrites! You are like whitewashed tombs, which look beautiful on the outside but on the inside are full of the bones of the dead and everything unclean. In the same way, on the outside you appear to people as righteous but on the inside, you are full of hypocrisy and wickedness. (Jesus, Matthew 23:27–28)

You, therefore, have no excuse, you who pass judgment on someone else, for at whatever point you judge another, you are condemning yourself, because you who pass judgment do the same things. Now we know that God's judgment against those who do such things is based on truth. So, when you, a mere human being, pass judgment on them and yet do the same things, do you think you will escape God's judgment? Or do you show contempt for the riches of His kindness, forbearance and patience, not realizing that God's kindness intended to lead you to repentance? But because of your stubbornness and your unrepentant heart, you are storing up wrath against yourself for the day of God's wrath, when His righteous judgment will be revealed. (Paul, Romans 2:1–5)

Okay, so maybe that was more than a few. These passages, these verses, are pulsating with absolute truth. Yes, God's mercy is great. His amazing grace is amazing. But we cannot fool God into believing that he doesn't know the honest truth of your heart and your willingness to deny the very life vest he has offered you as you slowly drown in your ignorance to the truth of God's commands and impending day of his wrath.

Am I trying to scare you? Damn straight I am. This is not something to be toyed with.

Let me be absolutely clear here: these words, these convictions, do not come from *me*! These convictions come from God's Word. He is *not* all butterflies and peach cobbler. He is God and he is to be feared. We should *all* have the fear of God in us. Not the kind of fear we would have for a boogey man or Jason Voorhees or Freddy Krueger, but the God who created you, called you, chose you, and you *cannot* choose to walk away. This is truly *life or death* here.

And I am trying to *wake up* the people. *Now* is the time, now is the place, to get right with God. That has to be number one over your kids, your wife, your dog, your money. God has to be number one, and if he isn't, then who is? What is?

Life is just too short to gamble on.

> Why is our generation so unhappy? Because there are many choices of temporary substitutes that we use to fill the void that only God can satisfy. (Lei Vallejo)

> In every heart there is a throne and a cross. If Jesus is on the throne, you must be on the cross. But, if you are on the throne, Jesus must be on the cross. (Unknown)

Read that last one again, and let it seep in deep into your understanding.

God loves you *passionately*. There is *no doubt* about that. He gives us all a million chances to change the direction of our ship into the light of the Son. But many miss the depths of the ocean that must be crossed. There is a purpose behind the plan of God. You must learn how to trust that, believe in that, like a child believes in Santa Claus. He is only as real as you choose to make him. Not make believe because God is as real as it gets. Trust me when I say this because I have heard his voice twice. Not in some book (but I have read so many things that has increased my faith dramatically through books), not in a sermon, and again, so much has been learned and taught and felt deeply through the thousands of sermons I have listened to over the last fifty years with so many tears I couldn't count. No, I tangibly heard God's voice calling me to follow and obey twice.

This book would not be written if I chose to live my life haphazard and casually chose to serve God when I felt like it. Or not as it should be but only for my benefit. *My* will be done on earth as it is *not* done in heaven. And yes, at many times in my life, this was me. I was extremely lost, but God never stopped looking for me and finding me. I was broken, but he never stopped fixing me. I was hopeless, but he never stopped encouraging me. I was selfish, self-centered, egotistical, self-aware, bloated, and full of addiction. Yet he kept calling my name. My only part in this is that I kept coming back to him, crawling on my hands and knees, face down in a puddle of tears, resentful of my actions, repentant of my sins, hopeless in my life, and knew that he was the only way I was ever going to find a way out of my pain, my sin, my rebelliousness.

> Therefore, as God's chosen people, holy and dearly loved, clothe yourselves with compassion, kindness, humility, gentleness and patience. Bear with each other and forgive whatever grievances you may have against one another. Forgive as the Lord forgave you. And over all these virtues put on love, which binds them all together in perfect unity. (Paul, Colossians 3:12–14)

Jesus has forgiven me, and this is just a guesstimate—at least 23,459 times throughout my life.

I jest, but truthfully, this is pretty accurate. I have been redeemed. I have been saved. I have been rescued. I have been enlightened. I have been pardoned. I have been forgiven. I have been set free from the chains of my bondage of sin and addiction. I have been chosen because I *never* stopped seeking after the heart of Jesus. Pouring myself into him even when the storms were beating the hell out of me, Jesus was *always there* reaching his hand through the crest of the water below the waves reaching for me to save me once again and give me another chance at life, another chance to live like Christ.

I remember as a kid when my mom would take us to the fair, and we would only get so many tickets to ride the rides. And once they were gone, that was it. The fun was over. No more tickets, no more rides. Jesus only has so many tickets for each of us to ride into heaven. Please take the tickets and make sure you get on that ride that leads to eternal life; time is running out. The tickets are running out.

> Jesus fed 5,000 but only 500 followed Him after lunch. He had 12 disciples but only 3 went further in the garden, and only one stood with Him at the Cross. The closer you get to the Cross, the smaller the crowd gets. (Unknown)

> Satan's greatest weapon is man's ignorance of God's Word. (A. W. Tozer)

> In a large house there are articles not only of gold and silver, but also of wood and clay; some are for noble purposes and some for ignoble. If a man cleanses himself from the latter, he will be an instrument for noble purposes, made holy, useful to the Master and prepared to do any good work. Flee the evil desires of youth, and pursue righteousness, faith, love and peace, along with those who call on the Lord out of a pure heart. (Paul, 2 Timothy 2:20–22)

It is never too late to say, "I am sorry." Never too late to say, "Please forgive me."

We *all* screw up, we *all* make mistakes, no one is immune to human failure, and Jesus knows this all too well. He is our ambassador, our Counselor, our Redeemer, and our Friend. He came to earth to be one of us, so when he fulfilled the mission, he could be the one to represent us to the Father. This should be so reassuring and bring you so much peace. He *loves us* that much. We are chosen!

Do not shine so that
others see you but so that through you
others can see Him.

—C. S. Lewis

CHAPTER 10

Jesus Freak

The deepest level of worship is praising God through the pain,
thanking God during the trials, trusting Him when we're tempted
to lose hope, and loving Him, even when He seems distant.
At my lowest, God is my Hope. At my darkest, God is my Light.
At my weakest, God is my Strength. At my
saddest, God is my Comforter.
—Unknown

There are rare Christians whose very presence incites others
to be better Christians. I want to *be* that rare Christian.
—A. W. Tozer

If you are seeking the Lord, you will be tempted. You will be
trialed by Satan. And the Lord will allow it to a certain degree…
but don't think by coming to the Lord Jesus everything is
going to be smooth, all problems are going to be solved, no.
If you're thinking this way, you're mistaken. See, when you
come to the Lord Jesus, He may not change your situation,
but definitely one thing He will do…He will change you.
See, if the Lord changed every situation that you went through…
He has done you no favor. Why? Because you never grew. You never
grew in your spirituality, you never grew in wisdom, you never
grew in strength. He just fixed the situation and, you didn't go

> through the hard labor in order to become a man. You remained
> that little weak baby in your spiritual life and your Christian life.
> So when you ask the Lord to fix a situation…He may or
> may not change it…but definitely…He *will change you*…
> to make you stronger so next time when a problem comes
> you can withstand it and overcome it. Now this is absolute
> beauty…because the Lord wants you to come to Him…
> and the only way He is going to get you to come to Him
> is when He makes you grow and become a man.
> —Bishop Mar Mari Emmanuel

It is safe to say, after coming this far in the reading of this book, I would assume to believe you would classify me as an absolute Jesus freak. And you are correct.

It is also safe to say, I have been called many names because of this choice, this life choice to follow the Rabbi and do my best to imitate him. I will *never* be him, but if I can shine some of his light and add some of his salt to this bland world in darkness, then I have done my duty. I have fulfilled the call.

It is and should be considered an honor to be called a Jesus freak.

Because of the deafening challenges to live this way, you will have many enemies and naysayers who only want to pick you apart, point out your faults and mistakes, and do everything they can to shine a dark shadow over you simply because you are doing the opposite of what is cool or right in the eyes of fallible man.

Let me make something very clear in the pursuit of following Jesus. You no longer can be one who wants to please man or to follow and please this world, but it will take a complete 180-degree turn to be a slave to Christ. A servant to emulate Jesus in every possible way.

> Since, then, you have been raised with
> Christ, set your hearts on things above, where
> Christ is seated at the right hand of God. Set
> your minds on the things above, not on earthly

> things. For you died, and your life is now hidden
> with Christ in God. (Paul, Colossians 3:1–3)

A life transformed can only be explained within the parameters of the one who has been transformed. Those on the outside looking in struggle to make sense of someone who would be willing to give up everything to follow after Jesus. But this is exactly what happens. Most lives that are lived are lived outwardly and with the intention of comfort, relaxation, success, wealth, entertainment, and or a life filled with stuff, materialism, and self-absorption. "It's all about me. I create my own existence, and all that happens is within my own power. I earned it; therefore, it is mine."

A follower of Christ becomes someone focused, not of this world, but they set their hearts on things above. Choosing to share the gospel with anyone willing to listen, choosing to love everyone despite our differences, seeking after a heart of Christ, and choosing to forgive those who have hurt them, along with asking for forgiveness of those who they have hurt. Choosing to understand the things you have, the money you possess, are not yours but God's. Choosing to let go of all that you believe is in your control and handing it over to God, who is really in control. You are no longer of this world. But are already looking forward to when you can go home to be with the Lord. You become kingdom-minded. Seeking after what will bring glory to God and no longer to yourself.

This does not mean we are excusing ourselves from the world we are currently living in or are choosing to become nomads living in caves and eating locusts. No, for those who truly choose to become followers of Christ, it means we are choosing to pick up our cross and to lay down our lives for others, thinking of others before ourselves. Living a life of servanthood to others with the love and sacrifice of Jesus Christ.

> For the message of the cross is foolishness to
> those who are perishing, but to us who are being
> saved it is the power of God. For it is written: I
> will destroy the wisdom of the wise; the intelli-

gence of the intelligent I will frustrate. (Paul, 1 Corinthians 1:18–19)

Many who walk in the world walk according to that of the world. They follow their desires, their own commands, and they follow those who fulfill what they believe to be complete. Politics, sports, success, career, toys. All eventually become a false reality—a false joy, a false relationship, a false understanding of what they believe to be true. And when that world comes crashing down around them, they seek out another faction of falsehood, continuously rotating from one desire, one sin to the next, until one day, their life of selfishness is over, death comes calling, and their fear of death and what awaits them becomes too much to handle.

Let's be real, life is extremely difficult. Those who may have read some, or all, of my other books have come to know how much adversity I have had to fight through and how much work God has had to do in me to bring me to this humble man standing before you. Or more accurately, writing before you.

If we so choose to please man instead of pleasing God, we will be empty and void of the most important relationship you could ever have. Men/women will disappoint you, hurt you, abandon you, wreck you. Trust me, I know. I have been on the receiving end of too much of this throughout my life. But that is on me. My bad. My poor choices. I chose me over God. I chose women over God. I chose sex over God. I chose everything over God, and I suffered deeply and tremendously. It was painful, horrid, and gut-wrenching to go through over and over again. All the while, God is sitting on the sidelines yelling at me, "How is that working for you?"

A little over three years ago in Uganda, I stood before a clean water well surrounded by at least three hundred Ugandans of all ages.

That well serves over a thousand people with fresh, clean, naturally filtered water, which is extremely difficult to find in Africa. And because I chose to follow Jesus and because he chose to call me, I obeyed and was able to be a part of something so incredibly special. I stood there looking into the eyes of these children, healthy and happy, full of smiles and energy, just being kids. This clean water well meant they no longer had to worry about the disease that was making them sick and killing them. They no longer had to spend twenty to thirty minutes scooping water one scummy, diseased scoop at a time; they could fill their jerry cans in twenty seconds and be on their way. They could go to school and learn without being sick or having to spend so much time away from school doing chores like fetching water. They could be kids. As I sat there looking into their beautiful brown eyes, I was flooded with an immense amount of love surging up from within and then it came pouring out in a flood of tears as I began to take in the reality of my choices to the obedience of Jesus. Treasures in Heaven Thrift store has now paid for and built sixty-five clean water cistern wells in Uganda in the last two years and seven months. *That* is God.

There is *no* greater feeling in the world than to know you are making a *huge* difference in someone else's life, especially to that of a child. I am a Jesus freak because of this right *here*! I am even crying as I am writing this because of the impact it had on my life then and continues to impact me now.

This world and all it offers you is garbage in the eyes of Christ. What matters is loving each other and loving God. When it becomes about you and your glory, you lose.

> Love must be sincere. Hate what is evil; cling to what is good. Be devoted to one another in brotherly love. Honor one another above yourselves. Never be lacking in zeal, but keep your spiritual fervor, serving the Lord. Be joyful in hope, patient in affliction, faithful in prayer. Share with God's people who are in need. Practice hospitality.
>
> Bless those who persecute you; bless and do not curse. Rejoice with those who rejoice; mourn with those who mourn. Live in harmony with one another. Do not be proud but be willing to associate with people of low position. Do not be conceited. Do not repay anyone evil for evil. Be

> careful to do what is right in the eyes of everybody. If it is possible, as far as it depends on you, live at peace with everyone. Do not take revenge, my friends, but leave room for God's wrath, for it is written: "It is mine to avenge; I will repay," says the Lord. "If your enemy is hungry, feed him; if he is thirsty, give him something to drink. In doing this, you will heap burning coals on his head. Do not be overcome by evil, but overcome evil with good." (Paul, Romans 12:9–21)

Radical Christianity will challenge you like never before. It is an expulsion and a removal of who you once were and then allowing God to start the process of healing you from all of your past and from within.

I have heard one hundred stories of the miraculous healing of Jesus through the lives of so many people who struggled with addictions. Jesus broke their chains. They are free men and women because they put their trust in Jesus. When you experience this kind of deep spiritual healing and experience, you will never be the same.

You instantly become a Jesus freak. You almost can't even help it. The supernatural power you feel throughout your body and soul is an overwhelming feeling of God's love and forgiveness and acceptance, and it is simply without an explanation of words. I have been there, and I have felt this power, this healing. And it is the coolest thing you will ever experience. Once you have been filled with the Holy Spirit at the moment you genuinely accept Jesus into your heart, you are forever changed. Your life will never be the same.

The true seeking of a Christ-filled heart is to be seeking with a thirst that only Jesus can quench. When this world comes to end, Jesus will finish the work he started. He is the Alpha and the Omega, the beginning and the end. No amount of good will get you into heaven if you don't even believe in the Son of God. If you truly want to be saved, come to him and seek him with your whole heart. Thirst for the righteousness of God. Turn away from what this world has to offer, which is eternity in hell. The door is wide open; all you have to do is walk through it and choose to believe.

I just watched an interview with three young women who looked to be in their early twenties. These women were randomly picked at what looks like to be in a shopping mall. They were then asked a few questions: "Do you believe you would go to heaven?"

They all answered "Yes," because they all believed that they were good enough to get into heaven.

He continued asking, "Have you ever told a lie? Have you ever stolen anything? Have you ever looked at a man with lust? Have you ever had sex outside of marriage?"

All serious questions. And most of those questions were met with a yes. Then the interviewer told them, "According to the Ten Commandments, you would all be guilty when you stand before Jesus on Judgment Day."

But then he gave them the good news. He asked them, "What did God do for you so that wouldn't have to go to hell? Do you know?"

They answered, "He died."

"That's right, yes, Jesus came here two thousand years ago and really did die on that cross for you and for me." Then he said to the young women, "I am also a good person but full of sin. I also need Jesus. What he did for us is he sacrificed himself so that we can be made whole. Sin requires a sacrifice and so someone had to come and pay the price, pay that penalty for our sins. So God sent his Son, Jesus, who lived a sinless life. He lived a perfect life for all of our sins."

By now, these women's facial expressions looked like they had just been slapped with a sixteen-inch trout. With this uncomfortable line of questioning and some seriously hard truth, this was either becoming a very difficult pill to swallow or they were feeling totally convicted. Not sure which one or both.

He goes on to say, "I want you to think of it like this: if you are in a courthouse and somebody comes in and legally pays your fines, the judge can then let you go, right? Well, it is the same thing with God. When you allow Jesus to pay for your sins, God can let you into heaven. Does that make sense?"

And they answered, "Yes, it does. It does make sense."

He goes on to say, "Okay, Romans 10:9 says, 'That if you confess with your mouth and believe in your heart that Jesus is Lord of your life and that God raised him from the dead, you will be saved."

The video ends there, and I did not get to see the result of that conversation, but I found this very interesting because of how their face expressions and body language had changed so drastically throughout the questions and conversation. When he first started asking them the personal questions like "Are you a liar, a thief, have you had sex outside of marriage, etc.?" They were giggling and smiling, answering yes to these questions, but it didn't take long for their mood to change.

I found it most interesting that one of the women to the far left was seriously struggling with this line of questioning the most. It wasn't the questions as much as it was hearing the truth of her lifestyle. I could tell she was feeling very convicted, almost sad to the reality of it all. Almost embarrassed would be more accurate, and she probably was.

Imagine how this would feel if you had to stand before Jesus and answer these questions? Imagine if you went to church every Sunday as far back as you could remember, youth group too, summer Bible camp, and now you are in college and your lifestyle has no representation of Jesus at all. None. In fact, most, if not all, of your friends don't even know you are a Christian. At least, this is who you think you are deep down because of your upbringing. Your parents were Christians, so then you must be. I mean, you went to church. You do *believe* in God. But do you live *for* Him? Does He know *you*? Do you even own a Bible? If so, do you even read it?

> There are two types of Christians. Those who believe in God, and those who sincerely believe they believe. (Girolamo Savonarola)

These are not trick questions. These are very serious questions, just like the man who was interviewing random women in a mall somewhere in rural America.

Some of those women knew that Jesus had died for them, but sadly, it obviously didn't matter much, did it?

Good is *not* enough. But somewhere along the way, through the very shallow waters of our Americanized Christianity, we have somehow come to believe that Jesus doesn't really mean what he says. He is too loving and caring and would never hurt anyone.

Hmm, that is not the Bible I am reading.

People, mostly those who are atheists, hate the idea that a good and loving God would even grasp the idea that he can and would throw people into hell for choosing to not believe in his Son, Jesus. Now I don't know about you, but what I have read many times is just that. Warning after warning after warning. How many warnings do you need to have in print? Either those who don't know this *never* read the Bible or they simply skim over what might hurt their feelings.

Throughout scripture by way of God's prophets and writers, he has instructed humanity how to live and how not to live. God has given us warnings of the consequences to those of us who reject his ways and choose to live our lives apart from his instructions. Here are a few scriptural examples.

In John 3:36, John the Baptist warns us about the consequences of choosing to not follow Jesus or believe in him. It states, "Whoever believes in the Son has eternal life, but whoever rejects the Son will not see life, for God's wrath remains on him."

Mark 9:42–48 states, "And if anyone causes one of these little ones who believe in me to sin, it would be better for him to be thrown into the sea with a large millstone tied around his neck. If your hand causes you to sin…cut it off. It is better for you to enter life maimed than with two hands to go into hell, where the fire never goes out. And if your foot causes you to sin, cut it off. It is better for you to enter life crippled than to have two feet and be thrown into hell. And if your eye causes you to sin, pluck it out. It is better for you to enter the kingdom of God with one eye than to have two eyes and be thrown into hell, where 'The worms that eat them do not die, and the fire is not quenched.' Everyone will be salted with fire."

From these verses comes some startling language. First to address the caution of harming little ones in the faith. This is expressed and fully applies both to what we do individually as teachers and leaders in our examples to those who are being led and taught, and this would also apply in what we allow to fester in our Christian fellowship. Our thoughts and actions must be motivated by love.

Jesus also used some crazy verbiage while explaining in great detail the importance of cutting sin out of our lives. The process of discipline in our life choices will be painful but incredibly worth it if we are to take seriously the true following of Jesus. This will involve ending a relationship, a job, giving up a habit that is against God's will for your life. It will feel as painful as losing a hand or a foot or an eye.

But overall, it is the pursuit of becoming righteous in the eyes of God, and it would be worth the sacrifice to choose Jesus over what the world wants or even what we would want. He has to become number 1 in your life. Nothing can stand in the way of faith. We must be ruthless in removing sins from our lives now in order to avoid being stuck with them for eternity.

And finally, the worm and fire and to the Jews, they represent both internal and external pain. What could be worse than that?

> For the wages of sin is death, but the free gift of God is eternal life in Christ our Lord. (Paul, Romans 6:23)

> The Lord is not slow to fulfill His promise as some count slowness, but is patient toward you, not wishing that any should perish, but that all should reach repentance. (2 Peter 3:9)

> But as for the cowardly, the faithless, the detestable, as for murderers, the sexually immoral, sorcerers, idolaters, and all liars, their portion will be in the lake that burns with fire

and sulfur, which is the second death. (Jesus, Revelation 21:8)

To step into the unknown is a scary step indeed. It takes courage to not lean anymore on your own understanding but to choose to trust in a God that cannot be tangibly seen or touched. But this is exactly where God wants us to go. Like the old trust fall where you fall back into the arms of others off a chair or steps, only God will not drop you, He is ready to catch you. God is not some fairy tale from a distant time in a galaxy far, far away. He is just as relevant now as he was two thousand years ago. Jesus is alive, and he is kicking the hornet's nest. There are revivals happening all over the world, and God is showing up in many places and taking names. I believe it is time for an uprising of Jesus freaks all over this country and this world to make themselves known; we are tired of being silent. It is time to stand up and shout to the world: Jesus is Lord of lords and King of kings! Hallelujah!

> We always thank God, the Father of our Lord Jesus Christ, when we pray for you, because we have heard of your faith in Christ Jesus and of the love you have for all the saints—the faith and love that spring from the hope that is stored up for you in heaven and that you have already heard about in the word of truth, the gospel that has come to you.
> All over the world this gospel is bearing fruit and growing, just as it has been doing among you since the day you heard it and understood God's grace in all its truth. For this reason, since the day we heard about you, we have not stopped praying for you and asking God to fill you with the knowledge of His will through all spiritual wisdom and understanding. And we pray this in order that you may live a life worthy of the Lord and may please Him in every way: bearing fruit

in every good work, growing in the knowledge of God, being strengthened with all power according to His glorious might so that you may have great endurance and patience, and joyfully giving thanks to the Father, who has qualified you to share in the inheritance of the saints in the kingdom of light.

For He has rescued us from the dominion of darkness and brought us into the kingdom of the Son He loves, in whom we have redemption, the forgiveness of sins.

He is the image of the invisible God, the firstborn over all creation. For by Him all things were created: things in heaven and on earth, visible and invisible, whether thrones or powers or rulers or authorities; all things were created by Him and for Him. He is before all things, and in Him all things hold together. And He is the head of the body, the church; He is the beginning and the firstborn from among the dead, so that in everything He might have the supremacy. For God was pleased to have all His fullness dwell in Him, and through Him to reconcile to himself all things, whether things on earth or things in heaven, by making peace through His blood, shed on the cross.

Once you were alienated from God and were enemies in your minds because of your evil behavior. But now He has reconciled you by Christ's physical body through death to present holy in His sight, without blemish and free from accusation—if you continue in your faith, established and firm, not moved from the hope held out in the gospel. This is the gospel that you heard and that has been proclaimed to every creature under heaven, and of which I, Paul, have become a servant. (Paul, Colossians 1:1–23)

Holy Moses, that was *amazing*! *This* right here what you just read is *exactly* the full description of how I would describe a Jesus freak. By the way, the title "Jesus freak" is actually a wonderful compliment. I can only hope and pray that this becomes a title with which I am blessed to be called.

But these verses from Colossians are simply breathtaking. They cover the full complexity and depth of not only who Jesus is but how we should look upon him and worship him as our Lord and Savior. Wow. Well said, Paul, well said.

Can't wait to meet that guy. That will be an incredible moment only second to Jesus.

I have often pondered the depths of what it truly means to follow Christ, and I have done my best to cover them in my books. How deep does the rabbit hole go? In my personal opinion, I believe the rabbit hole never ends. The pursuit of Christ on this earth over a lifetime would never be enough. That is what makes this journey so exciting, so adventurous, and so worth the choice to be chosen.

My journey has been excruciatingly painful, but through that pain, I became compassionate and empathetic to others' pain. I understand and I can feel their pain, and this is most likely why I cry so easily for another who is dealing with their struggle. This is a part of how God allowed me to become the man I am and then used my pain to further his kingdom to bring him glory. Amazing.

I believe to the extent of pursuing Jesus with all your heart and all your mind and all your strength, you will become enamored by him, and in the process of falling in love with Jesus, he reveals to us what is specifically for us and the purpose he created us for. And in that process, in that journey, if you keep the faith and are diligent about what it means to be a follower of Christ, picking up your cross daily, losing your life for the sake of Christ so you can find it, you will become a Christian and Christlike, a Jesus freak.

So many people, so many religions, throw around the title of Christian like it is a party favor. Like it is a title anyone can get or you can be born with it. To be Christlike means to take on the sufferings of Christ, and I would presume there aren't many lining up to get crucified, let alone be whipped thirty-nine times.

But do not underestimate the probability that there will be great suffering, as there already has been for centuries simply because you love Jesus. The sacrifices are many, the sufferings inevitable, to surrender it all to him, painful, but is it worth it? One thousand times over, it is worth it. Why? Because of the reward that awaits us, the crown that awaits us, the treasure that awaits us, all that equals up to eternity with Jesus. Cha-ching!

I asked Google, "Approximately how many people have died for Jesus Christ and the faith?" and this is what Google said, "We estimate that more than seventy million Christians have been martyred over the last two millennia, more than half of which died in the twentieth century under fascist and communist regimes. We also estimate that one million Christians were killed between 2001 and 2010 and about 900,000 were killed from 2011 to 2020" (Christian Martyrdom—Gordon Conwell Theological Seminary).

No more tears, no more pain, no more disease and no more death. Life eternal with the Lord.

It doesn't get any better than that. And that, my friends, is why I would die for Jesus in a heartbeat.

> Do nothing out of selfish ambition or vain conceit. Rather, in humility value others above yourselves, not looking to your own interests but each of you to the interests of the others. (Paul, Philippians 2:3–4)

> If you're called to preach and teach the Gospel, you WILL be sifted for the wisdom that anoints your message. If you are called to empower, your self-esteem will be attacked—your successes hard fought. You're calling will come with spiritual warfare and a sifting...*both* are necessary for your mantle to be authentic,

humble and powerful. "Your crushing won't be easy because your assignment is not easy. You can't minister *powerfully* what you haven't walked out. Read that sentence again. When you're feeling the weight of it coming down on you, *run* to the Father who longs to be your comfort. Let Him whisper your true identity over you while resting under the shadow of His wings. Position yourself against His heartbeat. Let Him renew your strength and set your eyes forward. No olives, no oil. No grapes, no wine. Your oil is not cheap my friend. (Hannah Williamson)

Amen.

Jesus's teaching was radically different than what we expect. His is an upside-down kingdom where life is found in death, power is found in weakness, freedom comes with surrender, greatness is found in service, the first will be last and the last first, and the enemies are to be loved and not hated."

—Author unknown

CHAPTER 11

Sacrifice

Then He said to them *all*: "If anyone would come after me, he must deny himself and take up his cross daily and follow me."
—Jesus, Luke 9:23

Be imitators of God, therefore, as dearly loved children and live a life of love, just as Christ loved us and gave himself up for us as a fragrant offering and sacrifice to God.
—Paul, Ephesians 4:23

Just so you know, I was done writing this book with just the thirteen chapters I had already completed, and then this morning, I opened Facebook and finally read a story I kept seeing. The post features a picture of a very old house, run-down. and from the looks of it, home of a poor family with children standing in the doorway. I decided it was time to read the caption. Little did I know that it would jump-start me into adding another chapter to this book. But this is how God works. And with that introduction, I must include this story since it brought tears streaming down my face. I hope it touches your heart as much as it touched mine.

It was Christmas Eve 1942. I was fifteen years old and feeling like the world had caved in on me because there just hadn't been enough money to buy me the rifle that I'd wanted for Christmas.

We did the chores early that night for some reason. I just figured Daddy wanted a little extra time so we could read in the Bible. After supper was over, I took my boots off and stretched out in front of the fireplace and waited for Daddy to get down the old Bible.

I was still feeling sorry for myself, and to be honest, I wasn't in much of a mood to read scriptures. But Daddy didn't get the Bible; instead, he bundled up again and went outside. I couldn't figure it out because we had already done all the chores. I didn't worry about it long though, I was too busy wallowing in self-pity.

Soon he came back in. It was a cold clear night out and there was ice in his beard. "Come on, Matt," he said. "Bundle up good, it's cold out tonight." I was really upset then. Not only wasn't I getting the rifle for Christmas, now he was dragging me out in the cold, and for no earthly reason that I could see. We'd already done all the chores and I couldn't think of anything else that needed doing, especially not on a night like this. But I knew he was not very patient at one dragging one's feet when he'd told them to do something, so I got up and put my boots back on and got my coat. Mommy gave me a mysterious smile as I opened the door to leave the house. Something was up, but I didn't know what.

Outside, I became even more dismayed. There in front of the house was the work team, already hitched to the big sled. Whatever it was we were going to do, it wasn't going to be a short, quick, little job. I could tell. We never hitched up this sled unless we were going to haul a big load.

SURRENDER

Daddy was already up on the seat, reins in hand. I reluctantly climbed up beside him. The cold was already biting at me. I wasn't happy. When I was on, Daddy pulled the sled around the house and stopped in front of the woodshed. He got off and I followed.

"I think we'll put on the high sideboards," he said. "Here, help me." The high sideboards! It had been a bigger job than I wanted to do with just the low sideboards on, but whatever it was we were going to do would be a lot bigger with the high sideboards on.

Then Daddy went into the woodshed and came out with an armload of wood—the wood I'd spent all summer hauling down from the mountain, and then all fall sawing into blocks and splitting. What was he doing? Finally, I said something. I asked, "What are you doing?"

"You been by the Widow Jensen's lately?" he asked. Mrs. Jensen lived about two miles down the road. Her husband had died a year or so before and left her with three children, the oldest being eight. Sure, I'd been by, but so what?

"Yeah," I said. "Why?"

"I rode by just today," he said. "Little Jakey was out digging around in the woodpile trying to find a few chips. They're out of wood, Matt." That was all he said and then he turned and went back into the woodshed for another armload of wood. I followed him. We loaded the sled so high that I began to wonder if the horses would be able to pull it. Finally, he called a halt to our loading. then we went to the smoke house and he took down a big ham and a side of bacon. He handed them to me and told me to put them in the sled and wait. When he returned, he was carrying a sack of flour over his right shoulder and a smaller sack of something in his left hand.

"What's in the little sack?" I asked. "Shoes, they're out of shoes. Little Jakey just had gunny sacks wrapped around his feet when he was out in the woodpile this morning. I got the children a little candy too. It just wouldn't be Christmas without a little candy."

We rode the two miles to Mrs. Jensen's pretty much in silence. I tried to think through what Daddy was doing. We didn't have much by worldly standards. Of course, we did have a big woodpile, though most of what was left now was still in the form of logs that I would have to saw into blocks and split before we could use it. We also had meat and flour, so we could spare that, but I knew we didn't have any money, so why was he buying them shoes and candy? Really, why was he doing any of this? Widow Jensen had closer neighbors than us; it shouldn't have been our concern.

We came in from the blind side of the Jensen house and unloaded the wood as quietly as possible then we took the meat and flour and shoes to the door. We knocked. The door opened a crack and a timid voice said, "Who is it?"

"Lucas Miles, ma'am, and my son, Matt, could we come in for a bit?"

Mrs. Jensen opened the door and let us in. She had a blanket wrapped around her shoulders. The children were wrapped in another and were sitting in front of the fireplace by a very small fire that hardly gave off any heat at all. Mrs. Jensen fumbled with a match and finally lit the lamp.

"We brought you a few things, ma'am," Daddy said and set down the sack of flour. I put the meat on the table. Then he handed her the sack that had the shoes in it. She opened it hesitantly and took the shoes out one pair at a time. There was a pair for her and one for each of the children—sturdy shoes, the best, shoes that would last. I watched her carefully. She bit her lower lip to keep it from trembling and then tears filled her eyes and started running down her cheeks. She looked up at my Daddy like she wanted to say something, but it wouldn't come out.

"We brought a load of wood, too, ma'am," he said. Then turned to me and said, "Matt, go bring in enough to last awhile. Let's get that fire up to size and heat this place up." I wasn't the same person when I went back out to bring in the wood. I had a big lump in my throat, and as much as I hate to admit it, there were tears in my eyes too. In my mind, I kept seeing those three kids huddled around the fireplace and their mother standing there with tears running down her cheeks with so much gratitude in her heart that she couldn't speak.

My heart swelled within me and a joy that I'd never known before filled my soul. I had given at Christmas many times before, but never when it had made so much difference. I could see we were literally saving the lives of these people.

I soon had the fire blazing and everyone's spirits soared. The kids started giggling when Daddy handed them each a piece of candy and Mrs. Jensen looked on with a smile that probably hadn't crossed her face for a long time. She finally turned to us. "God bless you, she said. "I know the Lord has sent you. The children and I have been praying that he would send one of his angels to spare us."

In spite of myself, the lump returned to my throat and the tears welled up in my eyes again. I'd never thought of my Daddy in those exact terms before, but after Widow Jensen mentioned it, I could see that it was probably true. I was sure that a better man than Daddy had never walked the earth. I started remembering all the times he had gone out of his way for Mommy and me and many others. The list seemed endless as I thought on it.

Daddy insisted that everyone try on the shoes before we left. I was amazed when they all fit and I wondered how he had known what sizes to get. Then I guessed that if he was on an errand for the Lord that the Lord would make sure he got the right sizes.

Tears were running down Widow Jensen's face again when we stood up to leave. My Daddy took each of the kids in his big arms and gave them a hug. They clung to him and didn't want us to go. I could see that they missed their daddy and I was glad that I still had mine.

At the door he turned to Widow Jensen and said, "The Mrs. wanted me to invite you and the children over for Christmas dinner tomorrow. The turkey will be more than the three of us can eat, and a man can get cantankerous if he has to eat turkey for too many meals. We'll be by to get you about eleven. It'll be nice to have some little ones around again. Matt, here, hasn't been little for quite a spell." I was the youngest. My two brothers and two sisters had all married and had moved away.

SURRENDER

Mrs. Jensen nodded and said, "Thank you, Brother Miles. I don't have to say, May the Lord bless you, I know for certain that He will."

Out on the sled I felt a warmth that came from deep within and I didn't even notice the cold. When we had gone aways, Daddy turned to me and said, "Matt, I want you to know something. Your mother and me have been tucking a little money away here and there all year so we could buy that rifle for you, but we didn't have quite enough. Then yesterday a man who owed me a little money from years back came by to make things square. Your mom and me were real excited, thinking that now we could get you that rifle, and I started into town this morning to do just that, but on the way I saw little Jakey out scratching in the woodpile with his feet wrapped in those gunny sacks and I knew what I had to do. Son, I spent the money for shoes and a little candy for those children. I hope you understand."

I understood, and my eyes became wet with tears again. I understood very well, and I was so glad Daddy had done it. Now the rifle seemed very low on my list of priorities. He had given me a lot more. He had given me the look on Mrs. Jensen's face and the radiant smiles of her three children. For the rest of my life, whenever I saw any of the Jensens or split a block of wood, I remembered, and remembering brought back that same joy I felt riding home beside of my daddy that night. He had given me much more than a rifle that night, he had given me the best Christmas of my life. (Harvey Patterson)

This story is a perfect example of when we stop to think about the word *sacrifice*. This act, among many others I have touched base on, is an act of will. It is in the pursuance of something beyond our natural instinct to survive. Naturally and sadly, we most definitely seek out our own needs and wants before others. We tend to take care of "me" before "we" in most situations and in most circles of life. Now, this isn't to say that there are many, many chances and opportunities where we choose the right path of generosity and do the right thing. A lot of us do. And that is awesome. But sadly, it has almost become a fad or a way to be recognized and applauded when we see an opportunity to help someone and then purposely choose to have the opportunity recorded so as to make it shown to the world your acts of kindness or sacrifice.

This does not make it right. This is a selfish act to promote oneself, and it is sad.

I will admit that throughout my life, I have struggled at times to focus on others before myself, thinking that this was perfectly normal to think of myself before the needs of others. But it didn't take me long to figure out how this can have damaging effects on not only my heart and soul, but through the eyes of the people closest to me. The fruit of my selfishness shone brightly around me, and it was rotten fruit. Even more crushing was knowing that God knew my true intentions and saw clearly my selfish heart. Conviction was not far behind, and the truth of the gospels eventually penetrated my heart and soul and began to revive my hardened heart to see more clearly how deep and how wide and how beautiful it is to give to others in their time of need.

True sacrifice comes in many forms and through many acts of love and kindness.

In the fall of 2006, in Uganda, Africa, I came into the full understanding of this act of sacrifice, and I was shaken to my core. I soon understood as I looked into the eyes of these children, suffering in the poorest of poor, that something had to be done. I was teleported out of myself and into the open arms of Christ who held me there in that mud-and-stick hut with his love and forgiveness as I shed so many tears I could not count. My heart broke again and again and again each time as I looked into the eyes of brokenness, children whose parents had died from AIDS, children, only twelve years old, who became heads of households over their younger siblings to care for them and find a way to feed them. Thousands upon thousands of children orphaned or dying because of malnutrition, diseased water, malaria, and diarrhea.

The pain so deep and devastating, it broke me.

Jesus wanted me to see this; this is what he called me to back in 2004. I heard his voice in church, and he wanted me to go to Uganda to see this, to know this, to understand this. And since then, it has been my honor to listen and obey, to follow and carry my cross, to sacrifice whatever it took to fulfill the calling and purpose to which Christ had called me to. To do *whatever* was needed to be done to make a difference in the lives of these children and their families.

I am only telling you this so I can paint a picture of what it means to choose, to sacrifice. Most of the time, when an opportunity arises where you can choose to sacrifice something for someone else, it is not planned or is expected. It is usually an opportunity that arises unexpectedly where you can radically do something beautiful for someone else. I love these opportunities, not to be seen or to be proud, but to be the example of Jesus of love, of kindness, of giving, of changing just a little bit more, to be like Jesus. But even more important is to see how your love and act of kindness touches the soul of the one being loved upon with kindness and generosity. It is priceless and it is heavenly.

Every act of kindness can slowly set you free.

This is why I love the movie *It's a Wonderful Life* so much. I am brought to tears *every time* I watch it. Its message runs so deep into my heart and soul that it is simply too difficult for me to not cry tears of absolute joy.

Our world, sadly, seems to be moving in the wrong direction if you haven't already noticed. I do believe that God is sifting his people. Sifting the sheep from the goats. And it is scary.

Twice now, God has asked me to let go of things I collected such as vintage Star Wars toys and other collectibles to show my allegiance to the greater picture to not allowing things of this world to become more important than that which is way more important. And that is to give of what we have to those who have not.

Jesus Speaks to the Rich Young Man

Now a man came up to Jesus and asked, "Teacher, what good thing must I do to get eternal life?"

"Why do you ask me about what is good?" Jesus replied. "There is only One who is good. If you want to enter life, obey the commandments."

"Which ones?" the man inquired.

Jesus replied, "Do not murder, do not commit adultery, do not steal, do not give false testimony, honor your father and mother, and love your neighbor as yourself."

"All these I have kept," the young man said. "What do I still lack?"

Jesus answered, "If you want to be perfect, go, sell your possessions and give to the poor, and you will have treasure in heaven. Then come, follow me."

When the young man heard this, he went away sad, because he had great wealth.

Then Jesus said to His disciples, "I tell you the truth, it is hard for a rich man to enter the kingdom of heaven. Again, I tell you, it is easier for a camel to go through the eye of a needle than for a rich man to enter the kingdom of God."

When the disciples heard this, they were greatly astonished and asked, "Who then can be saved?"

Jesus looked at them and said, "With man this is impossible, but with God all things are possible."

Peter answered Him, "We have left everything to follow you! What then will there be for us?"

SURRENDER

> Jesus said to them, "I tell you the truth, at the renewal of all things, when the Son of Man sits on His glorious throne, you who have followed me will also sit on twelve thrones, judging the twelve tribes of Israel. And everyone who has left houses or brothers or sisters or father or mother or children or fields for my sake will receive a hundred times as much and will inherit eternal life. But many who are first will be last, and many who are last will be first." (Jesus, Matthew 19:16–30)

There have been many days when I had to stand on this truth to fulfill the calling God put on my heart. Sacrificing is painful; it hurts, and it goes against our selfishness, our pride, and the way of the world.

Have you noticed that when choosing to follow Christ, we have chosen to do the opposite of what most people do or want to do? In fact, everyone who wants to live a godly life in Christ Jesus will be persecuted. This is not exactly a vacation that anyone wants to jump on board and be a part of, but Jesus did say, *"Count the cost."* When someone chooses to be a follower of Jesus, God's moral laws have already been written on their hearts and so our consciences have already been preprogrammed to understand right from wrong. In the process of accepting Jesus into our hearts and lives, the Holy Spirit also becomes a part of us, which in turn will compel us toward living a righteous life.

The sin doesn't magically stop, but the Holy Spirit guides us and convicts us of the sin that needs to stop, and as we grow in our relationship with Christ, we will become more aware of our sin and the desire to do and obey what Jesus asks us to do.

To choose to sacrifice our own lives, our time, our money, our gifts, our own possessions and even our own families to do the will of the Father is extremely challenging, but the reward is treasure in heaven.

Trials and tribulations are inevitable. God will allow these to happen so we can grow and become more like his Son. And in those opportunities to be the fruit of the Spirit and sacrifice for the sake of others and for the sake of Jesus. This is where we get to see and feel the magnitude of giving. Our hearts grow inside our chests; love wells up inside of you and changes you bit by bit, tear by tear. And you soon realize that *the* most important thing is to *be* Jesus in these moments.

It is obvious who sacrificed the most for all of us in his willingness to give his life for ours. His example screams vehemently from the cross, and through his sacrifice, it has changed the course of history as nothing else has. In the pursuit of truly surrendering our lives to Christ and sacrificing our lives, however and whatever that may be, I can pretty much guarantee you that the opportunity to serve and to sacrifice for God's kingdom will arise, and God will most likely put this situation in your path for a reason. I would even go on to say if serving and sacrificing are currently not in your faith journey or haven't been, then your faith may be nothing but lip service.

Sacrifice has become a big part of my life. I look for it. I long for it. I hope every day that there will be opportunities where I can make a difference in every way possible, and it takes a bit of ingenuity. I believe it takes a complete change of heart, a twisting of the mind and an "outside of the box" mentality. When we have strongly pursued to know Christ, then we begin to see with Christlike eyes the world in front of us. We begin to understand and see clearly those who need our help. The scriptures come alive in front of us, and we soon realize that it is up to us to finish this race, obey the commands of God, and take care of the least of these—the homeless, the thirsty, the hungry, the naked, the orphans, the widows, those who are in jail, the broken-hearted, the lost, the addicts, the drunkards, the sinful, the hurt, and those who don't know Jesus—anyone of these who walk into your life and need your help. Do not hold on to the worldly possessions believing you can take them with you, but choose to store up treasures in heaven, for where your treasure is, there will your heart be also.

> I am convinced that anyone who brings up the question of consequences in the Christian life is only a mediocre and common Christian! I have known some who were interested in the deeper life, but began asking questions: "What will it cost me—in terms of time, money, in effort, in the matter of my friendships?"
> Others ask of the Lord when He calls them to move forward: "Will it be safe?" This question comes out of our constant bleating about security and our everlasting desire for safety above all else. A third question that we want Him to answer is: "Will it be convenient?"
> What must our Lord think of us if His work and His witness depend upon the security and the safety and the convenience of his people? No element of sacrifice, no bother, no disturbance—so we are not getting anywhere with God! We have stopped and pitched our tent halfway between the swamp and the peak. We are mediocre Christians! (A. W. Tozer)

> All you can take with you...is that which you have given away. (Peter Bailey, *It's a Wonderful Life* [1946])

It is quite the fragile god who needs political power to pressure and enforce their will. It is quite the powerful God who partners with peasants, is born in poverty, washes feet, heals the sick, advocates for the oppressed, is unjustly killed and still changes the entire world.

—Rev. Ben Cremer

CHAPTER 12

Endgame

So many have been terrorized by false teachings of the gospel. True teachings point to Christ! False teachings condemn your conscience. Stop sitting under the tutelage of spiritual abuse. When the gospel is weaponized…the saints have an adversary. Remember who hated Christ…who persecuted Christ… and who crucified Christ. It wasn't those identified as "sinners"…but rather those who thought themselves to be "righteous." Law righteousness *does not* save. Christ is the *only* reason we are no longer enemies with God."

—Louis Scott

I believe that one reason why the church of God at this present moment has so little influence over the world is because… the world has so much influence over the church.

—Charles Spurgeon

The end.

This used to be the sign that the movie you are watching is most definitely over, but I don't recall seeing this in movies anymore. Am I wrong?

The end is a peculiar thing in regard to real life. When the movie ends, that is usually it. You get up and head home or go to bed. But when it is actually the end or you know it is close to the end, everything seems a little more clarified, a little more tuned in, a little more clear. You become way more interested in making amends, finishing your bucket list, saying your goodbyes, if you get the chance. If you have time, you might want to pass along some words of wisdom to leave behind for the living. You ponder more seriously the thought of the afterlife and maybe even seek out forgiveness. And finally, you want all your loved ones to know how much you truly love them. And if you are waiting to die, suddenly, the skies seem bluer and the wind more beautiful as it sings you a song while it is whisking by you. The birds sound like an orchestra, and you don't want to miss a single little miracle that is taking place all around you in what seems like a slow-motion replay.

I would imagine that you would rethink your whole life, the things you did right and the things you did horribly wrong, the things you wished you would have done, and to do what you can with the time you have left, if willing and possible.

If you are a true follower of Christ, you look forward to the end because the end is not the end, but a new beginning that never ends.

The truth is we are all one more day closer to the end, closer to death. I am not trying to be grim here, just trying to be real. The endgame is not a game many want or choose to play. But it is inevitable. The game eventually ends. The real trick to all of this, though, is how well did you play the game of life?

> Make a tree good and its fruit will be good or make a tree bad and its fruit will be bad, for a tree is recognized by its fruit. You brood of vipers, how can you who are evil say anything good? For out of the overflow of the heart the mouth speaks. The good man brings good things out of the good stored in him, and the evil man brings evil things out of the evil stored up in him. But I tell you that men will have to give account on the day of judgment for every careless word they have spoken. For by your words you will be

acquitted, and by your words you will be condemned. (Jesus, Matthew 12:33–37)

The game of life should always be played with the endgame as the goal. How will you win in the end? What are my main objectives to seeing this through to the end? What really matters? How deep does the rabbit hole go?

There are definitely no guarantees in this life, which is a gift by the way. But we move forward anyway through our teen years thinking we now know everything. Our parents are idiots, and it is time to take our lives into our own hands now. "Now I am in charge." Until we step out into the big bad world and realize we are the idiots and "I have a lot to learn."

Death is a reality that no one wants to confront or even acknowledge. It is in a way, a taboo, a subject that is left out of the conversation at the dinner table or at the water cooler.

When it is brought up, it brings with it a manner of sadness, loss, grieving, and mourning. It is a difficult thing all together.

I have been spared by the sudden blow of death from anyone very close to me. I have lost my dad, to whom I was not very close to, sadly. I have lost all my grandparents, which again, I was also not close with them and not by my choice.

I have lost uncles, aunts, friends, and pets. Death touches the front door of every human being in one or many ways.

After my dad died in 1999, it took me years to eventually shed tears over the loss of him. It all of a sudden hit me as I was sharing my story with a bunch of men in a men's church group meeting, and I bawled like a baby.

There is a deeper issue I would like to step into—a subject much closer to what is truly important to the endgame. I am hoping that we can dive deeper into this chapter with a greater understanding of what is at cost here.

> The seed that fell among the thorns stands
> for those who hear, but as they go on their way

> they are choked by life's worries, riches, and pleasures, and they do not mature. (Jesus, Luke 8:14)

If you were to look back over your life and were to take a moment and count those who are no longer living, it would surprise you at how many you grew up with either watching on TV, movies, or listening to on the radio, that are no longer with us.

My wife and I, along with my two oldest children, recently went on a trip to Scotland. My wife and I were wasting time doing some sightseeing while our kids were at a concert. We stopped in and toured an old cemetery which was filled with tombstones twice the height of myself. Many of these tombstones were dated as far back as the 1600s, which kind of blew my mind, but also made me think of how many people so quickly pass away. There were some people who lived to a ripe old age and others who had only lived a year or two.

Life is surely fleeting and is like a brisk wind that comes in quickly and then is gone again.

One of the things that has always been imbedded into me, and I am not sure why but I have a guess, is that I have always been cognizant of life not being so long, but more of a time that stands still for only so long and then it is gone. In this pretext, it is then so extremely important that this life, this short blip in time should be valued worthy, and not only just worthy, but that it should be looked upon with great concern regarding the ending of this life. We must be cognizant and aware of the importance of how we do life, how we live, how we treat others, how we treat ourselves, our siblings, our friends, family, coworkers, and especially our children. How did we spend our time, our energy, our resources, our money, and what did we do with the gifts and talents given to us? Did we serve others in love and faith, or did we selfishly squander all the blessings given to us?

> All that the Father gives me will come to me, and whoever comes to me I will never drive away. For I have come down from heaven not to do my will but to do the will of Him who sent me. And this is the will of Him who sent me,

> that I shall lose none of all that He has given me, but raise them up at the last day. For my Father's will is that everyone who looks to the Son and believes in Him shall have eternal life, and I will raise him up at the last day. (Jesus, John 6:37–40)

We must understand to the greatest degree the importance of our immortal soul. Evil is present. It is easily seen and/or felt in the everyday existence of life. Even as a child, I could sense evil and knew it was real. And if evil is this present and alive, then the opposite is as well.

I will *never forget* when I was around fourteen to fifteen years old. I was hanging out with a friend at his house when his parents were gone, and we decided to raid his father's VHS collection to find a movie to watch. We decided that *The Exorcist* was the best choice. Bad, bad, choice. I couldn't sleep without fear and nightmares for two weeks. Don't ever watch that movie.

Yes, it is just a movie. And yes, it is makeup, special effects, and a story that is surely fabricated; although I totally believe in people being demon possessed, it was still just a movie. But what I will tell you is this, I *knew* deep down that what I was watching and experiencing was the closest I would ever get to seeing what is truly unseen in the demonic and evil spiritual world, Satan in his truest form.

There is something happening that is unseen, a war taking place for our very souls. This unseen force of both good and evil, God and Satan, is mingling in and among us. On one hand, God is fighting for us, encouraging us, filling us up with hope and love and forgiveness. On the other hand, the evil one is coercing us, tempting us with the tools and toys of man, with the sins of the flesh, the sins of greed, the sins of power and lust, and all the other means that lead to death to the very depths of hell where it is dark, a never-ending burning fire and forever separated from the Creator who loves you and gave everything for you, even free will to choose your destiny, and his Son as the greatest sacrifice. This tug-of-war will come to a head to the end of the world, which leaves us with the question: whose side are you on?

> He who is not with me is against me, and he who does not gather with me scatters. (Jesus, Matthew 12:30)

> Since then, you have been raised with Christ, set your hearts on things above, where Christ is seated at the right hand of God. Set your minds on things above, not on earthly things. For you died, and your life is now hidden with Christ in God. When Christ, who is your life, appears, then you also will appear with Him in glory. Put to death, therefore, whatever belongs to your earthly nature: sexual immorality, impurity, lust, evil desires and greed, which is idolatry. Because of these, the wrath of God is coming!
> You used to walk in these ways, in the life you once lived. But now you must rid yourselves of all such things as these: anger, rage, malice, slander, and filthy language from your lips. Do not lie to each other, since you have taken off your old self with its practices and have put on the new self, which is being renewed in knowledge in the image of its Creator. Here there is no Greek or Jew, circumcised or uncircumcised, barbarian, Scythian, slave or free, but Christ is all and is in all.
> Therefore, as God's chosen people, holy and dearly loved, clothe yourselves with compassion, kindness, humility, gentleness, and patience. Bear with each other and forgive whatever grievances you may have against one another. Forgive as the Lord forgave you. And over all these virtues put

SURRENDER

on love, which binds them all together in perfect
unity. (Paul, Colossians 3:1–14)

Now, once we have grasped a hold of this truth and have come to this conclusion, what do we do? With the knowledge of life and death standing before us, how do we proceed? If we have chosen to believe and accept Christ as our Lord and Savior, then what are the rules of the game? And how do I go about winning the endgame?

> All the forces of darkness cannot stop what
> God has ordained. (Isaiah 14:27)

Every single human being alive has used their own brain cells and thinking abilities to consider and ponder the universe, the earth spinning on its axis in the dead of space, the complexity of the human body and how it works, the science behind gravity and the air that we breathe, etc.

But the most important thing to ponder is the One who created us, the One who created it all!

When I was nine years old, I got on to my knees and prayed for Jesus to come into my heart and live with me. I sensed that this was good and that he loved me. It took many, many years to understand this concept truthfully and honestly. And I have been pursuing this Son of Man my entire life. I have found the one true faith. All others I knew by their fruit. My soul was not moved by any other than Jesus. I did not find any other faith-based religions truly seeking after the heart of the Creator.

Nothing is more important than this. Nothing.

> Ponder how valuable your soul must be for
> Satan to tirelessly pursue it, and the King to lay
> down His own life for it. (Unknown)

The endgame is to see who will win and who will lose. The battle over this universe, this great big blue ball in the sky and all its inhabitants, are the prize and God, our God, is doing everything He can to win souls and not lose any to the enemy.

The move you must take to win is to lose. Lose your life for the sake of Jesus Christ. To win in the end, you must humble yourself, take up your cross, deny your life, surrender it to Jesus, obey his will, and fulfill the purpose for which you were created. And then you will win. You will receive the prize and will be given a crown. And as you serve others in love and humility, you will store up for yourself treasures in heaven where no thief can steal, no moth destroys, nor rust attack and deteriorate your treasure.

> Nevertheless, God's solid foundation stands firm, sealed with this inscription: "The Lord knows those who are His," and, "Everyone who confesses the name of the Lord must turn away from wickedness." (Paul, 2 Timothy 2:19)

For our home is not of this world, but eternally set for us in heaven.

> Insecurity comes when we find our identity in anything but God. (TobyMac, #speaklife)

The world we are living in, in my opinion, is collapsing. It is collapsing socially, economically, financially, spiritually, scientifically, physically, and emotionally, to name a few. The true endgame, in my opinion, seems to be revealing the signs of the times, the end of days, *the end* of life as we currently know it.

Let me elaborate.

I am going to quote here some interesting dialogue with true biblical doctrine to give some insight on what the Bible says and how it relates to us.

Let's begin.

SURRENDER

The Rapture of the Church

There are four strong points in 1 Thessalonians that indicate the church will be exempt from the coming wrath of the tribulation.

A Promise of Deliverance

First, in 1 Thessalonians 1:9–10, exemption from the coming wrath of the tribulation is explicitly stated. "For they themselves report about us what kind of reception we had with you, and how you turned to God from idols to serve a living and true God, and to wait for His Son from heaven, whom He raised from the dead, that is Jesus, who delivers us from the wrath to come."

Notice in this verse that it is Jesus coming from Heaven who delivers us from the wrath to come. And the word "wrath" has the definite article in front of it. It's not just any wrath, but the wrath to come. This points to the specific time of wrath in the coming day of the Lord. Moreover, Jesus's coming for us is the means of our deliverance from the coming wrath of the tribulation. This strongly supports the pre-trib position.

First the Rapture

Second, in 1 Thessalonians 4:13–5:9, the order of events is striking. First Thessalonians 4:13–18 deals with the rapture of the church to meet the Lord in the air. Then, in 1 Thessalonians 5:1, a new subject is introduced by Paul with the words, "Now as to" (peri de in Greek). This Greek phrase is one of Paul's favorite ways in his letters to change subjects. So, it's clear that he is finished focusing on the rapture. But what is the next subject in 5:1–9? The day of the Lord or coming time of tribulation.

"Now as to the times and the epochs, brethren, you have no need of anything to be written to you. For you yourselves know full well that the day of the Lord will come just like a thief in the night" (1 Thessalonian 5:1–2).

Why is this significant? Because of the order of the events. Which event is mentioned first, the rapture or the tribulation? It's the rapture first, then the tribulation or Day of the Lord. The tribulation is pictured as a separate and subsequent event from the rapture.

The order is clear.

1 Thessalonians 4:13–18: The Rapture

1 Thessalonians 5: 1–9: The Day of the Lord (Tribulation)

The rapture and the day of the Lord can hardly be parts of the same event as post-tribulationists maintain. The rapture comes before the day of the Lord in 1 Thessalonians 4–5.

"You" and "Them"

Third, in 1 Thessalonians 5:1–5 the interplay between the different audiences is critical, yet easy to miss. Read 1 Thessalonians 5:1–5 and notice the pronouns that are in italics (you probably never knew someone could get this excited about pronouns).

"Now as to the times and the epochs, brethren, you have no need of anything to be written to you. For you yourselves know full well that the day of the Lord will come just like a thief in the night. While they are saying, 'Peace and safety!' then destruction will come upon them suddenly like birth pangs upon a woman with child; and they shall not escape. But you, brethren, are not in darkness, that the day should overtake you like a thief; for you are all sons of light and sons of day. We are not of night nor of darkness."

Notice the dramatic change in this setting between you and we (the believers) in the first and second person, and they and them (the unbelievers) in the third person. It's striking. The wording indicates that when the tribulation comes there will be two groups of people each exclusive of the other. One group will be raptured, and the other will face destruction. The day of the Lord will come upon them, and they shall not escape (5:3). Then in 5:4 there's a sudden contrast: "But you are not in the darkness." They stand in sharp contrast to the believers in vv. 4–11 who will escape. This clear distinction between the unbelievers, who will not escape, and the believers, who will escape, is another strong indication that believers are exempt from the wrath of the day of the Lord.

An Appointment to Keep

Fourth, 1 Thessalonians 5:9 says clearly, "For God has not destined us for wrath, but for obtaining salvation through our Lord Jesus Christ." This verse is clear that we have an appointment with salvation, not wrath. Some maintain that this simply means that believers are not destined for the wrath of hell, but that we will be saved. However, there are two reasons why I don't think that's what this verse is referring to.

First, the Thessalonians already knew they were not destined for God's wrath in hell. Paul had told them this very clearly in 1 Thessalonians 1:4. Second, in the context of 1 Thessalonians 5:1–8 what wrath has Paul just been talking about? Not the wrath of hell but the wrath of the tribulation or day of the Lord. In this context, that's the wrath that believers will be delivered from. As Walvoord says, "In this passage he is expressly saying that our appointment is to be caught up to be with Christ; the appointment of the world is for the day of the Lord, the day of wrath. One cannot keep both of these appointments." (Ralph Mark B. Malinao, The Rapture of the Church)

Just to be clear, I don't write these books to make money; in fact, I give them away. I also don't write them to try and make a name for myself. I could care less about that. I write them to share the greatest story ever told. It is *all about* Jesus and his redemption of man. I am writing these books to share the most incredible journey of God's love on this once broken, messed-up man, who has sinned and fallen into sin a thousand times, yet his mercy remains. Redemption is here for any walk of life. God loves you…period. It is only because of him that I am who I am now. Otherwise, I probably wouldn't like me very much. And I would still be stuck where I was thirty years ago.

> Death is no punishment to the believer: It is the gate of endless joy. (C. H. Spurgeon)

But God heeds his warnings that before you can enter into heaven, "No one comes to the Father except through me" (Jesus, John 14:6).

The time of grace is running out. Jesus is the only way, the only truth, and the only life worth investing your life into. The endgame is drawing near, and the end-time warnings are becoming stronger, the prophecies are starting to take shape and the time of grace, like I said, is running out. If we, as a nation, eject God from all of our businesses, our government, our schools, our sports, everything, then his blessings, his covering of this great nation will be gone. And that, my friends, is why you are seeing chaos, mass murders, suicide, crime, greed, corruption, fill in the blank, taking over our streets and causing unrest, stress, worry, anxiety, and so much pain.

Without God, you will see the likes of Sodom and Gomorrah or Ninevah where Jonah objected to go but was coerced in the belly of the whale, then was spat up upon the land, where he finally obeyed God and warned Ninevah, "Repent or your city will be overturned" (Jonah 2:10, 3:1–10).

But this is not only in America. It is all over the world.

Those of us who know God and are followers of Christ are watching, always watching to see what unfolds next. "I'm watching you, Wazowski. Always watching" (Roz, *Monsters Inc.*).

> But mark this: There will be terrible times in the last days. People will be lovers of themselves, lovers of money, boastful, proud, abusive, disobedient to their parents, ungrateful, unholy, without love, unforgiving, slanderous, without self-control, brutal, not lovers of the good, treacherous, rash, conceited, lovers of pleasure rather than lovers of God—having a form of godliness but denying its power. (Paul, 2 Timothy 3:2–5)

> And Jesus said, "Watch out that no one deceives you. For many will come in my name, claiming, 'I am the Christ,' and will deceive many. You will hear of wars and rumors of wars but see to it that you are not alarmed. *Such things must happen, but the end is still to come. Nation will*

rise against nation, and kingdom against kingdom. There will be famines and earthquakes in various places. All these are the beginning of the birth pains.

"Then you will be handed over to be persecuted and put to death, and you will be hated by all nations because of me. At that time many will turn away from the faith and will betray and hate each other, and many false prophets will appear and deceive many people. Because of the increase of wickedness, the love of many will grow cold, but he who stands firm to the end will be saved. And this gospel of the kingdom will be preached in the whole world as a testimony to all nations, and then the end will come." (Jesus, Matthew 24:4–14 [emphasis mine])

The Chosen, a phenomenal TV series, has now been viewed by over 550 million people worldwide and counting and is available in over 70 translated languages. Season 4 comes out in February 2024. It is *so* worth watching.

There simply is *no greater* step that can be taken, if not already done, than into the arms of Christ. When you have grasped completely the unending power and love of Jesus in your life, fear no longer lives, the chains of addictions have been broken, forgiveness has been given, and healing has taken place. The evil one has been vanquished and defeated by the only name that can win in this game called life, Jesus Christ. Amen and Hallelujah!

The endgame is all and in all the name of Jesus. He is the only source. He is the only way. He is the only truth. He is life. It is Jesus that brings forth those who will be the successors, the winners, the salt of the earth, the light in our world, those who have the courage to stand unashamed and proclaim to the world that Jesus is Lord of *all.*

First of all, you must understand that in the last days scoffers will come, scoffing and following their own evil desires. They will say, "Where is this 'coming' He promised? Ever since our fathers died, everything goes on as it has since the beginning of creation."

But they deliberately forget that long ago by God's word the heavens existed and the earth was formed out of water and by water. By these waters also the world of that time was deluged and destroyed. By the same word the present heavens and earth are reserved for fire, being kept for the day of judgment and destruction of ungodly men.

But do not forget this one thing, dear friends: With the Lord a day is like a thousand years, and a thousand years are like a day. The Lord is not slow in keeping His promise, as some understand slowness. He is patient with you, not wanting anyone to perish, but everyone to come to repentance.

But the day of the Lord will come like a thief. The heavens will disappear with a roar; the elements will be destroyed by fire, and the earth and everything in it will be laid bare.

Since everything will be destroyed in this way, what kind of people ought you to be? You ought to live holy and godly lives as you look forward to the day of God and speed its coming. That day will bring about the destruction of the heavens by fire, and the elements will melt in the heat. But in keeping with His promise, we are looking forward to a new heaven and a new earth, the home of righteousness.

So then, dear friends, since you are looking forward to this, make every effort to be found spotless, blameless and at peace with Him. (Peter, 2 Peter 3:3–14)

Concerning the coming of our Lord Jesus Christ and our being gathered to Him, we ask you, brothers, not to become easily unsettled or alarmed by some prophecy, report, or letter supposed to have come from us, saying that the day of the Lord has already come. Don't let anyone deceive you in any way, for that day will not come until the rebellion occurs and the man of lawlessness is revealed, the man doomed to destruction. He will oppose and will exalt himself over everything that is called God or is worshiped, so that he sets himself up in God's temple, proclaiming himself to be God.

Don't you remember that when I was with you, I used to tell you these things? And now you know what is holding him back, so that he may be revealed at the proper time. For the secret power of lawlessness is already at work; but the one who now holds it back will continue to do so till He is taken out of the way. And then the lawless one will be revealed, whom the Lord Jesus will overthrow with the breath of His mouth and destroy by the splendor of His coming. The coming of the lawless one will be in accordance with the work of Satan displayed in all kinds of counterfeit miracles, signs and wonders, and in every sort of evil that deceives those who are perishing. They perish because they refused to love the truth and so be saved.

For this reason, God sends them a powerful delusion so that they will believe the lie and so that all will be condemned who have not believed the truth but have delighted in wickedness.

But we ought always to thank God for you, brothers loved by the Lord, because from the beginning God chose you to be saved through the sanctifying work of the Spirit and through belief in the truth. He called you to this through our gospel, that you might share in the glory of our Lord Jesus Christ. (Paul, 2 Thessalonians 2:1–14)

For the Lord himself will come down from heaven, with a loud command, with the voice of the archangel and with the trumpet call of God, and the dead in Christ will rise first. After that, we who are still alive and are left will be caught up together with them in the clouds, to meet the Lord in the air. And so we will be with the Lord forever. (Paul, 1 Thessalonians 4:16–17)

While it looks like things are out of control, behind the scenes there is a God who has not surrendered His authority. (A. W. Tozer)

We are not saved by obedience, for obedience is the result of salvation. We are saved by faith because faith leads us to obey. (Charles Spurgeon)

God is not ashamed of the lowliness of human beings. God marches right in. He chooses people as His instruments and performs His wonders where one would least expect them. God is near to lowliness; He loves the lost, the neglected, the unseemly, the excluded, the weak and the broken.

—Dietrich Bonhoeffer

CHAPTER 13

Genuine Repentance

Of all acts of man repentance is the most divine. The greatest of all faults is to be conscious of none.
—Thomas Carlyle

No repentance is true repentance which does not recognize Jesus as Lord over every area of life.
—John C. Chapman

If we confess our sins He is faithful and just to forgive us our sins and to cleanse us from all unrighteousness.
—1 John 1:9

Genuine repentance must bear the seal of a corrected life.
—Lewis F. Korns

Ahh…repentance.

This has got to be in the top five most favorite things to do when it comes to our Christian walk. Not! Following in line with remorse, guilt, and shame, repenting is not always an easy task to accomplish. It means to humble yourself to the reality that you, once again, screwed up. We then have to bring our dark moments to the surface, face them, and then plead for mercy once again.

> Then Matthew held a great banquet for Jesus at his house, and a large crowd of tax collectors and others were eating with them. But the Pharisees and the teachers of the law who belonged to their sect complained to His disciples, "Why do you eat and drink with tax collectors and sinners?"
> Jesus answered them, "It is not the healthy who need a doctor, but the sick. I have not come to call the righteous, but sinners *to repentance.*" (Luke 5:29–32 [emphasis mine])

I googled the question: "How many times is repent/repentance mentioned in the New Testament alone?" Here is a great quote I found to sum it all up:

> Repentance is one of the foundation-stones of Christianity. Sixty times, at least, we find repentance spoken of in the New Testament. What was the first doctrine our Lord Jesus preached? We are told that He said, "Repent, and believe in the Gospel" (Mark 1:15).
>
> What did the Apostles proclaim when the Lord sent them forth for the first time? They "preached that people should repent" (Mark 6:12).
>
> What was the charge which Jesus gave to His disciples when He left the world? That "repentance and remission of sins should be preached in His name among all nations" (Luke 24:47).

> What was the concluding appeal of the first sermons which Peter preached? "Repent and be baptized. Repent and be converted" (Acts 2:38, 3:19).
>
> What was the summary of doctrine which Paul gave to the Ephesian elders, when he parted from them? He told them that he had taught them publicly, and from house to house, "testifying both to the Jews, and also to the Greeks, repentance toward God, and faith toward our Lord Jesus Christ" (Acts 20:21).
>
> What was the description which Paul gave of his own ministry, when he made his defense before Festus and Agrippa? He told them that he had taught all people that they should "repent and do works fit for repentance" (Acts 26:20).
>
> What was the account given by the believers at Jerusalem of the conversion of the Gentiles? When they heard of it they said, "Then God has also to the Gentiles granted repentance unto life" (Acts 11:18). (J. C. Ryle on repentance)

It is pretty clear to what extent the importance of repenting is in our continued relationship with Jesus.

Just the other night, right before bed, which is a normal custom of mine, I was feeling convicted and felt the need for repentance. I just sat there and kept saying I was sorry with tears rolling down my cheeks. But the beauty of this is how it feels after you have genuinely repented of your sins. You literally feel lighter, fresher, cleaner, and the air is fresh into your lungs as you take in deep breaths of relief and freedom from the sins that were bogging you down. Well, at least, this is how I feel.

In our house, we have a framed painting of the prodigal son, and it is beautiful. But the story is even more beautiful than the painting itself. It is one of the greatest stories told by Jesus with the act of repenting, surrendering, and forgiveness. I questioned whether I should put that story in this book, but then remembered that if Jesus shared this story, then so should I.

And it goes like this; read Jesus's words from the book of Luke:

> There was a man who had two sons. The younger one said to his father, "Father, give me my share of the estate." So, he divided his property between them.
>
> Not long after that, the younger son got together all he had, set off for a distant country and there squandered his wealth in wild living. After he had spent everything, there was a severe famine in that whole country, and he began to be in need. So, he went and hired himself out to a citizen of that country, who sent him to his fields to feed pigs. He longed to fill his stomach with the pods that the pigs were eating, but no one gave him anything.
>
> When he came to his senses, he said, "How many of my Father's hired servants have food to spare, and here I am starving to death! I will set out and go back to my father and say to him: Father, I have sinned against heaven and against you. I am no longer worthy to be called your son; make me like one of your hired servants." So he got up and went to his father.
>
> But while he was still a long way off, his father saw him and was filled with compassion for him; he ran to his son, threw his arms around him and kissed him.

The son said to him, "Father, I have sinned against heaven and against you. I am no longer worthy to be called your son."

But the father said to his servants, "Quick! Bring the best robe and put it on him. Put a ring on his finger and sandals on his feet. Bring the fattened calf and kill it. Let's have a feast and celebrate. For this son of mine was dead and is alive again; he was lost and is found." So they began to celebrate.

Meanwhile, the older son was in the field. When he came near the house, he heard music and dancing. So he called one of the servants and asked him what was going on. "Your brother has come home," he replied, "And your father has killed the fattened calf because he has him back safe and sound."

The older brother became angry and refused to go in. So his father went out and pleaded with him. But he answered his father, "Look! All these years I've been slaving for you and never disobeyed your orders. Yet you never gave me even a young goat so I can celebrate with my friends. But when this son of yours who has squandered your property with prostitutes comes home, you kill the fattened calf for him!"

"My son," the father said, "You are always with me, and everything I have is yours. But we had to celebrate and be glad, because this brother of yours was dead and is alive again; he was lost and is found." (Jesus, Luke 15:11–32)

Imbedded within this story are many delicate and intricate subjects that can be totally relatable even to this day, nearly two thousand years after this was initially told.

This story always brings me back to a time in the '70s and '80s when the movie *Jesus of Nazareth* would come on TV as a mini-series. This particular scene where Jesus ends up telling this story is so well done, as Jesus uses it as a metaphor in the explanation of how much Peter despises Matthew the tax collector for what he has done to the Jewish people and to the disgust and ridicule of his own family.

Peter hates Matthew with a passion, a very strong and bitter passion, and rightly so. But Jesus uses this story to explain how Matthew is the lost son and Peter is the older brother. As Jesus is telling this story while eating with tax collectors and sinners, Peter and the other disciples would not go into Matthew's house or they would be defiled.

So Peter sat in the doorway listening as Jesus was telling this story. And as Jesus got to the end of this story, Peter suddenly understood what Jesus was saying and entered Matthew's house, walking all the way up to Jesus and Matthew as now all three of them are standing together, with Matthew and Peter face-to-face and Jesus in the middle. Jesus brings them together into a brotherly bond of repentance, forgiveness, and love. Peter knew Jesus was referring this story to him and Matthew. Peter needed to repent of his judgment of his brother and see the beauty of the calling Jesus had made in asking Matthew to follow him and be one of his disciples.

It was a beautiful moment in surrendering to the will of Jesus who loves us and wants so much for us. The Father rejoices, as do the angels in heaven, when we repent of our sins, turn back to God, and surrender once again our lives to the Lord.

If there is no repentance, then there is no genuine act of surrendering to the will of Jesus, but only an act of selfishness and hypocrisy. A false witness and a false Christianity. Just because we have accepted Jesus into our hearts does not mean that our lives can just continue to be lived out in our sin-filled secular lifestyle.

There has to be a shift in the depths of your heart that shakes you to your core; you begin to long for righteous living and choosing to be an example of Jesus to the world. A light on a hill.

We will all fall down. We will continue to battle the sins of the flesh; that is inevitable, and this is why to repent is to once again bring back the focus of your life to Jesus who is the lover of your soul. Repent on your knees and give it to God so that you can once again allow Jesus to pick you back up and set you straight. He cleans the soul and then helps you on your way again. Amazing grace.

When I went through the Christian-based twelve-step program Celebrate Recovery years ago, one of the steps was to make amends with those with whom I hurt. I needed to find them, if possible, and ask for genuine forgiveness. To repent for my wrongdoing. This was a very difficult step for many of us to take but was so satisfying and well worth the time and energy it took to complete it.

Even as I am writing this chapter, I know of at least two people I need to make amends with and ask for forgiveness. One of those being my niece. I have struggled throughout my life with competitiveness and coming across too strong while playing card games or board games, even to the point of bullying and being belligerent. I blame my brothers though. I grew up with three of them, and you can only imagine the competition.

> Repentance is an inner change of heart and mind and an outward change of life. (John Blanchard)

> It is only through Christ that we can take full advantage of God's mercy and forgiveness through repentance in Jesus's name. (Monica Johnson)

To fall to your knees with arms open wide, tears streaming down your face, in full submission to the One who can redeem you with the blood he shed is truly one of the greatest, if not *the* greatest gift we have been given. This acknowledgment of your faults, your mistakes, your selfish motives, done with the act of obedience in repentance is truly a major part of surrendering it all at the foot of the cross.

With all that is going on in our world (which feels like a vacuum of evil penetrating every crevasse of our lives), I wonder how much more will God put up with. I wonder how deep all the evil will get as it constantly floods our thoughts and video screens with the nonsense of humankind at its worst. I strive to be a beacon of light, to be the salt of the earth, an open book of love and acceptance to every walk of life.

But I have to admit, it is becoming even more difficult to live out my faith with action, mercy, grace, and patience. I need Jesus every day and almost every minute of every day to calm the storm rising up within. I want to shout so loudly to those who are so lost in their fear and in their ignorance to the mind-meld of broken promises, evil leaders hell-bent on their selfish initiatives to grow their bank accounts through the devilish mishandling of information vital to making healthy decisions that affect millions, if not billions, of lives.

Is it not just me who is seeing so clearly the plans falling in place right before our very eyes put together by a dastardly plan of evildoers to fulfill the rapid decline of our once great America?

All that is happening is not by chance. It is a well-devised orchestra of demonic moves and greedy motives that has steamrolled us to the edge of oblivion. With all *that*, here is the good news, if and when this rollercoaster from hell ever stops, it will either be the beginning of the end (which is *really great news*) or it is *definitely* one giant leap toward the end, which I would personally accept with a glad heart.

As I have already said earlier in one of the prior chapters, none of us gets out alive anyway, so bring it on. I am not ignorant of what is taking place. And besides, if you are a child of God, the Holy Spirit is already preparing you for what is to come. I do *love* to see how many are finally fighting against the machine. People are starting to wake up and are seeing clearly and are finally calling what is truly bullsnot…bullsnot!

> Blessed are the poor in spirit, for theirs is the kingdom of heaven. (Jesus)

SURRENDER

> The Spirit of the Sovereign Lord is on me because the Lord has anointed me to preach good news to the poor. He has sent me to bind up the brokenhearted, to proclaim freedom for the captives and release from darkness for the prisoners, to proclaim the year of the Lord's favor and the day of vengeance of our God, to comfort all who mourn, and provide for those who grieve in Zion—to bestow on them a crown of beauty instead of ashes, the oil of gladness instead of mourning, and a garment of praise instead of a spirit of despair. They will be called oaks of righteousness, a planting of the Lord for the display of His splendor. (Isaiah 61:1–3)

From the Beatitudes comes the first of many *blessed*.

> Part of the understanding of the beatitudes is to see the Old Testament background concerning these descriptions of the Messianic kingdom and the people who enter it. With the mentioning of Isaiah 61:1–3…the Messiah would be anointed "To preach good tidings to the poor" (recall that in Luke 4…Jesus read that passage in the synagogue and said it was fulfilled in their hearing). That passage helps us a little with our understanding of "The Poor." We tend to think of the "poor" primarily in terms of finances or possessions. That is part of it, but there is a spiritual side to it too. The word Isaiah uses describes the people who had been taken into exile. They were of course poor, having their land and possessions ripped away; but they were also afflicted and oppressed, they were powerless and without hope, and they were desperate. The physical poverty was intensified by the poverty in their spirit.

The meaning of the text. The words that describe the poor in the Bible include these aspects, for the poor in Jesus' day had few possessions, were usually oppressed, had little power and less hope. They had no resources to fall back on; they had to depend on others for survival. Isaiah brought the people of his day good news—they would be delivered from bondage. But Jesus fulfilled that promise of bringing good news by proclaiming the gospel, the 'good news' of God. He did not make them rich in earthly possessions and power; but he fulfilled their greatest need.

People who are "poor in spirit" are those who are humble before God. They realize that they have nothing in this life that they can contribute to receiving the kingdom of heaven. They have afflicted their souls, meaning that they have humbled themselves and repented with deep contrition; and they have come to the king as helpless and hopeless sinners. There is no arrogance in them, no self-righteousness, no self-sufficiency. They are free from their own pretensions, and therefore they are free for God. Everyone who wishes to enter the kingdom must be "spiritually poor," for salvation is a gift from God.

And that is the good news for the genuinely poor and oppressed in this world. The poor person is not excluded because of his/her poverty; and the rich person is not accepted because of his/her wealth. Both must humble themselves before the Lord in order to be a part of the kingdom. It is often easier for the down and out of this world to do that, than for the rich to do it.

The blessing that Jesus announces is…"theirs is the kingdom of heaven." Now this of course does not mean that all poor people are in the kingdom. One thinks of the self-made poverty of the prodigal son. No, the poverty is not the chief thing, but the qualification of the spirit is. It is the poor in spirit, those who have humbled themselves and become dependent on God—they have the kingdom of heaven. In fact, everyone who is in the kingdom had to become poor in spirit.

They all come with a broken heart and a contrite spirit seeking the Savior.

Application. The clear lesson is that if any are going to enter the kingdom of heaven, they must become poor in spirit. This is the message of the kingdom; *it is the call of repentance.* They must humble themselves before God and acknowledge that they bring nothing of their own power, possessions or merit to gain entrance. Those who truly humble themselves and express their need of the Lord, they have the kingdom of heaven. And in this they find heavenly bliss.

So how does one become poor in spirit? The implication from the context preceding this is that one would hear the message of the kingdom and learn what kind of kingdom it is and how to enter it—*through repentance for sin and submission to the will of God.* The first step is to confess that by themselves they can do nothing, and then seek the gracious provision that God has made.

A secondary application would be to develop how this attitude is to characterize the attitude of the believers who are in the kingdom. They do not simply humble themselves to get in and then become self-sufficient (although some try to do it); they are to live their lives in *total dependence on God* to supply their needs. This will open the study to themes such as humility, faith, prayer, and obedience. (Allen Ross/Bible.org)

All in all, I do my very best to shine for my Savior, knowing full well that just around the corner is an opportunity to blow it. An opportunity to say the wrong thing, act the wrong way, respond with vulgarity, or to joke with a tainted taste of sin. Temptations usually come in the dozens, and this is one of our greatest challenges as we try so desperately to walk in the shadow of the Son of God, but we will fail and will fall. It is though not how much you failed or how hard you fell, but how you rebounded from those failures. God's mercy never ends; trust me, I know because I have tested his mercy, and it is beautiful. But do not abuse it or use it as a cash machine. God knows your heart, so lean on his grace and mercy, and when you slip up, acknowledge it, claim it, and genuinely repent of it, and on the day of judgment, you will be white as snow.

> Fallen man is not simply an imperfect creature who needs improvement: he is a rebel who must lay down his arms. Laying down your arms, *surrendering*, saying you're sorry, realizing that you have been on the wrong track and getting ready to start life over again from the ground floor—that is the only way out of a *hole*. This process of *surrender*—this movement is full speed astern—is *repentance*. (C. S. Lewis [emphasis mine])

Jesus didn't tell sinners to go to church…
He told His church to go to sinners.

—Author unknown

CHAPTER 14

I Surrender

Often I have heard people say, "How good God is! We prayed that it would not rain for our church picnic and look at the lovely weather!" Yes, God is good when he sends good weather. But God is also good when He allowed my sister, Betsie, to starve to death before my eyes in a German concentration camp. I remember one occasion when I was very discouraged there. Everything around us was dark, and there was darkness in my heart. I remember telling Betsie that I thought God had forgotten us. "No, Corrie," said Betsie, "He has not forgotten us. Remember His word: 'For as the heavens are high above the earth, so great is His steadfast love toward those who fear Him.'"

There is an ocean of God's love available—there is plenty for everyone. May God grant you never to doubt that victorious love—whatever the circumstances.

—Corrie Ten Boom

What comes into our minds when we think about God is the most important thing about us.
—A. W. Tozer

Here we are. This is where it all ends. The journey to get here was a simple act of God. I am unaware as to the results of this book and to its impact it has had on you…or not. That is not up to me. That is between you and God. I am just a messenger.

The responsibility rests on my shoulders to do the best that I can to make the content relatable, biblically sound, certain to hit you where it counts and at the right time. Realistically though, it is 90 percent God and 10 percent Don putting this context into play. I am just trying to relay what I feel the Holy Spirit is attempting to say and the importance of this information getting into the hands of those in whom God is trying to reach. I do believe time is running out.

There was another huge earthquake today in the world. This time in Nepal, so far, 150 dead. What is crazy though is that this was not headline news. It was way down on the list on the BBC newsfeed. Do you think it is this way, maybe, because it is becoming all too common in our world? The tragedies of our world, the natural disasters killing hundreds, if not thousands of people on a regular basis, is happening more and more often. Sounds a little too familiar with the warnings of the birth pains that Jesus spoke about in Matthew 24.

But what do I know? I am just a Jesus freak keeping watch over the outcomes of everyday life in the year 2023. It is almost weird to say it: the year 2023. It sounds like something straight out of a science fiction movie I watched as a kid.

I have covered a lot of ground over these last fourteen chapters, and I pray they were informative and helpful in the pursuit of finding some understanding and truth in the chaos we call planet earth. There are some people out there that would call me a conspiracy theorist, but honestly, I am just questioning everything simply because I can and we should. We can no longer trust very many people, especially the mass media and every social media construct. Ninety percent of what is out there is being directed by the ones who own most of the media and social media outlets. Spitting out their false narratives and extremely messed-up sexual gender dysphoria which has taken the world by storm.

> Questioning and doubting what's going on these days does not make you 'anti' anything. Nor does it make you a conspiracy theorist.

> Actually, questioning *is* and should be, the place of reason. The fact that questioning has become taboo, should, in fact, send a chill up everyone's spine. (Unknown)

But I digress. No doubt the world is a mess. But then again, it has been a mess for some time now. Truly no surprise there.

I have always done my best to try and be open-minded but keep one eye open to the shenanigans of a world so lost in its own selfishness. I want to stop and ponder that, which the world, mainly the extremist left liberals, find it so easily accepted as truth simply because a man or woman says so. These are just men, just women. Nothing else. To be ignorant to the possibility that greed has not seeped in and poisoned the hearts of so many people to do and say what the money has coerced them to say is simply ludicrous. This is the true virus that has poisoned too many and every walk of life. Disturbing to say the least, but not surprising.

When people put their trust in money, government, people of power, doctors and nurses, pharmacists, politicians, sports authority, newscasters, social media, etc., and choose to not trust in God first, you have set yourself up for some painful results.

> Do not love the world or the things in the world. If anyone loves the world, the love of the Father is not in him. For all that is in the world—the desires of the flesh and the desires of the eyes and pride of life—is not from the Father but is from the world. (1 John 2:15–16)

"Trust the science" has never been anything other than a marketing term that simply means "shut up and obey" and that doesn't sit well with me. In fact, I am scared to see the results of all the sheeple that just simply stepped forward without questioning a thing before taking the jab. It seems a lot of those results are already pouring in, and it is ugly.

SURRENDER

I can only pray that this may have awoken people to some of the craziness in our world. And to the fact we truly cannot trust much of anything anymore. I *only* trust in the God who loves me and my wife and my kids and maybe a few close friends.

This book has included a lot of subject matter to discuss and dissect. But hopefully, it has directed you to the main course, which is to surrender. This doesn't mean to surrender your life to the world that only wants to devour you or to that which will bury you but to surrender to the One who *truly loves you*—Jesus Christ.

Years ago, like twenty years ago, I prayed for something that might not make most people's top ten things to pray for. But I prayed for wisdom. I prayed for discernment, and I prayed for suffering, so I would be found worthy of living out my life genuinely for Jesus and to be like Jesus in every way.

Be careful what you pray for. It is for certain that to those he loves, he will refine through fire like gold is refined. And as a father disciplines his child, be prepared to be disciplined by the Father, for you are God's children.

Love will teach you the way, as long as you accept the way you are being loved. There is no purer love than that of Jesus. And if you choose to follow him, with all of your heart and soul, then you need to understand that to do so means you will need to purify yourself through fire, purify yourself through letting go of what you hold dear in this world and the worldly possessions you currently have. You need to surrender all things under heaven to Jesus.

If they come before Jesus, then Jesus is not your Lord, whatever you cherish is.

> My command is this: Love each other as I have loved you. Greater love has no one than this, that he lay down his life for his friends. You are my friends *if you do what I command.* (Jesus, John 15:12–14 [emphasis mine])

> If the world hates you, keep in mind that it hated me first. If you belonged to the world,

> it would love you as its own. *As it is, you do not belong to the world,* but I have chosen you out of the world. *That is why the world hates you.* (Jesus, John 15:18–19 [emphasis mine])

To surrender is to be free of the weight of this world, handing over the 150-lb. dumbbells to Jesus who is strong enough to handle it. The freedom alone is priceless when you choose to surrender that which you cannot control.

Today at church, and it has been a while since my wife and I had gone, I could barely get through one worship song and the tears started falling. The tears pour out of me not because of guilt and shame, but because of his redeeming blood.

The cross signifies the greatest act of love ever given to a bum like me or to all the ragamuffins in the world who don't feel like it, deep down, that they deserve to be loved like Jesus loves you and me.

The tears were uncontrollable, and once again, my heart was made whole, refreshed, and cleansed by the blood of Jesus.

You see, the sin never stops. We continue to make mistakes and fall into sin no matter how pure and perfect we want to be. It is inevitable but can be toned way down from a ton to only a few each day. But even those few sins still haunt me, and I must come before Jesus and get on my knees once more and wash his feet with my tears. It is in his great mercy and grace that I am overwhelmed and flooded within my soul from head to toe, and now, I can only whisper in worship because my voice is gone with the lump in my throat as I am enveloped in the arms of Christ.

I have surrendered once more, and it is the most beautiful thing you can ever feel and comprehend.

The weight of this world is heavy. The bag in which we haul over our shoulder carrying all the stress, all the responsibility, our jobs, bills, family errands, daily issues, concerns, worries of the world, politics, the stock market, retirement, car problems, children, parents, a clean house, and what to make for dinner. The list goes on and on. Day in and day out, we wrestle with our faith, we wrestle to make time for God, to not just read God's Word but to *spend time with*

God in his Word. We struggle to find time or remember to pray and then our prayer over dinner turns into a Sunday night prayer session.

To surrender your life, your *whole* life, to Jesus encapsulates a very strategic set of movements and decisions. Choices that we don't want to make or accept. We are, in a sense, unlocking the handcuffs from each of the things we struggle to control. We must unlock and let go of control over our money, and that means *all of it*, not just some. We must *believe* that not only can God be trusted, but that he knows best. It is like looking up to our fathers as kids and trusting him when we were learning to ride a bike that he wouldn't let go, but he did, and we learned to ride our bike without his help. On this occasion, we would no longer have to worry about our money because God is now in charge of that and all the other worries and responsibilities, we choose to let go.

I picture myself drowning in a lake of my own sin as I shove an arm out of the water with a huge stick in my hand with a white flag draped around it, flapping in the wind. I surrender, Lord, I surrender.

As believers in Christ, we must not fear, but learn to give our entire lives over to the Lord of our lives.

> God is love. Whoever lives in love lives in God, and God in him. In this way, love is made complete among us so that we will have confidence on the day of judgment, because in this world we are like Him. There is no fear in love. But perfect love drives out fear, because fear has to do with punishment. The one who fears is not made perfect in love. (1 John 4:16–18)

When we have stepped out of this world and into the reality of *who* Jesus truly is and not just a magical genie who we call upon only in distress or in dire need, but to engage in a deep and trusting relationship, diving deep into wanting to know the Son of God, only then can you begin to see clearly, when the veil is taken away, a friend who longs to show you and give you so much more than what we think we know. We are jettisoned into a place of absolute joy, complete safety, and a life that could never be imagined.

Each day we wake up is truly a blessing. If you can breathe, it is a blessing. If you can run, it is a blessing. If you can see the colors of a rainbow, it is a blessing.

Blessings, little miracles, are everywhere. I believe everyone has a chance to do something amazing every day, as long as they are looking for that chance and then capturing it when it is ready. Life is truly only as good as you see it, only as beautiful as you choose to find it, and that there is truly good in the world if you choose to believe it.

To surrender is to jump off a cliff without knowing what is below but trusting a friend when he says, it is the greatest jump you will ever take because when you jump and trust in Jesus, your faith grows, and you begin to fly, not fall.

This life, if you allow it, will punish you, beat you down, devour you, and try to destroy you. And many who call themselves Christians are feeling this kind of beat down and are not sure why. To die to oneself is to take upon your shoulders the cross of Christ. It is to make a choice to say that this life is no longer yours, but it is Jesus's life. It is a willingness to say to God, "I am yours…send me." Whatever your dreams, whatever your visions, plans, ideas, you surrender them to Jesus because you want to do his will and not your own. It is your sacrifice on the cross, you are picking up your cross, denying yourself, and giving up your life to fulfill the purpose that Jesus chose you for. Because if you truly understand following after Jesus, this means it is time to be kingdom minded. Focused on the great commandment. And being doers of the Word.

If you love me, you will obey what I command. And I will ask the Father, and He will give you another Counselor to be with you forever—the Spirit of truth. The world cannot accept Him, because it neither sees Him nor knows Him. But you know Him, for He lives with you and will be in you. I will not leave you as orphans; I will

> come to you. Before long, the world will not see me anymore, but you will see me. Because I live, you also will live. On that day you will realize that I am in my Father, and you are in me, and I am in you. Whoever has my commands and obeys them, he is the one who loves me. He who loves me will be loved by my Father, and I too will love him and show myself to him. (Jesus, John 14:15–21 [emphasis mine])

In that last verse, last sentence, Jesus says, "And I too will love him and show myself to him." Yes, you read that correctly. He will show himself to you, to me, to anyone who truly loves him, trusts in him, and has a relationship with him.

What does a relationship look like to you?

If you do not invest in an earthly relationship, that relationship usually falls away or falls apart and disintegrates. It does not take a highly intellectual human being to understand the concepts of fulfilling a true and deep relationship with someone. In marriage, you have to sacrifice a lot and unselfishly think of your spouse before yourself to have a healthy and long-lasting relationship that burns with a fire that will never be put out. Jesus wants this kind of relationship with you. He wants so badly to reconcile us to the Father where sin has built a ravine. Jesus wants to build a bridge so we can know the Father through him, his Son—*relationship.*

"If you love me..." If? I don't think there is anything to question here or to try and look any deeper than what is so plainly on the surface. *"You will obey my commands." If...if...*you love me.

So which is it? We cannot twist this around, mix it up or scan over this simple yet very strong point. You either want a relationship or you don't. That's it.

> Then He said to them all: "If anyone would come after me, he must deny himself and take up his cross daily and follow me. For whoever wants to save his life will lose it, but whoever loses his

life for me will save it. What good is it for a man to gain the whole world, and yet lose or forfeit his very self? If anyone is ashamed of me and of my words, the Son of Man will be ashamed of him when he comes in his glory and in the glory of the Father and of the holy angels." (Jesus, Luke 9:23–26)

Bam...man, I love the scriptures.

> If this present life is most important to you, you will do everything you can to protect it. You will not do anything that might endanger your health, safety or comfort. By contrast, if following Jesus is most important to you...you may find yourself in an unsafe, unhealthy, or uncomfortable situation or places. You will risk death, but you will not fear it because you know that Jesus will raise you to eternal life. Nothing material can compensate for the loss of eternal life. (Tyndale House Publishers Life Application Bible, 1991, Note Page 1818, Luke 9:23–26)

The scriptures paint a very detailed, very descriptive picture of what is asked of us, of those who want to follow the Rabbi. There is a very good reason Jesus asked us to count the cost before choosing to accept him as their Lord and Savior and to follow him, taking up our cross daily.

Who wants to lose their life? Anybody? Any takers? This is the challenge. This is the part of the story where it becomes a bit blurred, a bit skewed, and even becomes nonessential. Because those who see a benefit in choosing to become a Christian see one thing as important—a lifeline, a free ticket, a key that they can put on their key ring when it becomes necessary to use it. But the reality is the salvation of Christ is not a "get out of jail free" card, it is a cross. And Jesus is asking us to climb up that tree, sacrifice this life for the sake of the kingdom and for Jesus, and after you have done so, come and follow him.

Yes, salvation is a free gift, unearned, and free of having to do works to earn it, but Jesus makes it very clear that once you choose him, then it is time to get to work. And there are a lot of people who want to just sign a contract without having to read the contents of the contract or fulfill the requirements of the contract. The fence that you might be sitting on because you are indecisive if you want to follow Jesus or not is nonnegotiable. Jesus doesn't allow lukewarm Christians.

> I know your works: you are neither cold nor hot. I wish you were either one or the other! So, because you are lukewarm—neither hot nor cold—I am about to spit you out of my mouth. You say, "I am rich: I have acquired wealth and do not need a thing." But you do not realize that you are wretched, pitiful, poor, blind and naked. I counsel you to buy from me gold refined in the fire, so you can become rich; and white clothes to wear, so you can cover your shameful nakedness; and salve to put on your eyes, so you can see.
>
> Those whom I love I rebuke and discipline. So be earnest, and repent. Here I am! I stand at the door and knock. If anyone hears my voice and opens the door, I will come in and eat with him, and he with me.
>
> To him who overcomes, I will give the right to sit with me on my throne, just as I overcame and sat down with my Father on His throne. He who has ears to hear, let him hear what the Spirit says to the churches. (Jesus, Revelation 3:15–22)

I believe this message is of the utmost importance for all to hear, know, and to act upon now before it is too late. The scriptures need to be read, need to be heard, and need to be acted upon and made known. The end is right at our fingertips, and the results of our actions and our words, our very heart and soul, will steer us in the direction of our destination. You are either for him or against him.

> Whoever is not with me is against me, and whoever does not gather with me scatters. (Jesus, Matthew 12:30)

> For the time will come when men will not put up with sound doctrine. Instead, to suit their own desires, they will gather around them a great number of teachers to say what their itching ears want to hear. They will turn their ears away from the truth and turn aside to myths. (Paul, 2 Timothy 4:3–4)

The scriptures, when well-read and studied, and with the help of the Holy Spirit and teachers who are chosen to make them more plainly understood become our lifeline not only to the Father but also to his Son. They begin to meld with your spirit and penetrate your hardened heart so that Jesus can truly come in and live within you to help you on this incredibly difficult journey to become more like himself. Jesus, Paul, Peter, John—none of these guys ever said it would be easy, but totally worth it. The endgame is not only having the most incredibly beautiful adventure here on earth, but to be a beacon of light for those who are also lost that you may be able to guide them to the One who will not only save their soul but to give them peace and a hope beyond all understanding. A peace and a hope that subsides into your very being, which then produces an abounding love that can be given over and over again, producing an immense amount of care, generosity, patience, perseverance, kindness, truth, wisdom, compassion, trust, and *love*.

> This is the message we have heard from Him and declare to you: God is light; in Him there is no darkness at all. If we claim to have

> fellowship with Him yet walk in the darkness, we lie and do not live by the truth. But if we walk in the light, as He is in the light, we have fellowship with one another, and the blood of Jesus, His Son, purifies us from all sin.
>
> If we claim to be without sin, we deceive ourselves and the truth is not in us. If we confess our sins, He is faithful and just and will forgive us our sins and purify us from all unrighteousness. If we claim we have not sinned, we make Him out to be a liar and His Word has no place in our lives. (1 John 1:5–10)

And it continues:

> My dear children, I write this to you so you will not sin. But if anybody does sin, we have One who speaks to the Father in our defense—Jesus Christ, the Righteous One. He is the atoning sacrifice for our sins, and not only for ours but also for the sins of the whole world.
>
> We know that we have come to know Him if we obey His commands. The man who says, "I know him,' but does not do what He commands is a liar, and the truth is not in him. But if anyone obeys His Word, God's love is truly made complete in him. This is how we know we are in Him: Whoever claims to live in Him must walk as Jesus did." (1 John 2:1–6)

If you have to, *read that again*. Read it aloud so you can *hear* it. Read it until you know it. Read it until you understand it thoroughly. This is not a test. This is not a contract. This is life or death. Heaven or hell. Love or hate. Jesus or Satan. Good or bad. Eternity of endless pain and suffering with weeping and gnashing of teeth or an eternity of absolute love and joy that we cannot possibly fathom. I cannot make it any plainer than that.

> You are not too dirty for God to cleanse. You are not too broken for God to fix. You are not too far for God to reach. You are not too guilty for God to forgive. And you are not too worthless for God to love. (Unknown)

> Don't gamble with eternity. Hell has no exit doors. The moment we take our last breath, there will be no re-do's. Seek the Lord while He may be found. (Unknown)

When I was in rural Uganda for the first time back in 2006, the one thing that blew my mind and was the cause of so many tears of joy was watching and experiencing, feeling deep inside me the hope and love that the people of Uganda had within themselves, the relationship that was so genuine, so deep, and so real with their Lord and Savior, Jesus Christ.

They had nothing but were rich. They were so poor but had the most important thing of all. *The hope of what is to come.*

Our Americanized Christianity has diminished a lot of what Uganda has. A deep longing to have God be number one in every area of their lives. To truly walk with their Lord. To take up their cross and follow him. To trust him solely for their every provision. This is simply because they have no other distractions. They have nothing that comes before Jesus. And the simple reliance and trust of Jesus was profound for their very lives.

Everyone in Uganda has seen death. It is rampant over there because of the AIDS pandemic that hit them hard along with malaria and the sickness or death from dysentery and diarrhea from the lack of clean water. No bathrooms, no hygiene, nothing. It is all exposed to everyone, yet the Holy Spirit was felt more powerfully there than anywhere I have ever been. This is why I shed so many tears, thousands of tears, because of how these people *got him*. They understood what following and believing in Jesus truly meant. They had experienced suffering to the greatest degree, and since they knew suffering and had a relationship with Christ, they were hand in hand with their Savior.

It was the most beautiful thing I had ever seen. I knew then why Jesus spoke to me in church that day. He said, "Go to Uganda," and I went and have never been the same since. I probably wouldn't be writing this book right now if I had not obeyed his calling on my life or, even better, his commands.

Jesus is calling you even if you do not tangibly hear him or see him. He is there right at the door, knocking. He is calling to you through this book, these words, his Word. I am but a messenger, a conduit, a servant to bring the Good News of Jesus to anyone who may be listening.

Jesus came for the lost, the hurting, the lonely, the broken, the abused, the downtrodden, the lepers, the addicted, those with too much pride, or those who think that they are unloved or believe that they could not be forgiven for their track record is too dark. He came for the brokenhearted. He came for all the ragamuffins. He came for Matthew, the tax collector; Mary Magdalene, the prostitute; Paul, the hunter and killer of Christians…*this* is who he came for. He even came for Judas who would even betray him! All of us, for this is us. Do not turn away from the greatest gift you could ever receive, for it is priceless. Call on his name. Get on your knees or do what I did: lay face down on the floor or carpet or dirt, and surrender it all to Christ. *Surrender it all*, so you no longer have to carry the burden of life, the burden of death, and what happens after we die.

It is an honor to share this truth with you. I hope you see the value in the words I am attempting to create, so the true picture is revealed. God is at the center of all of this, every part. He is here in every way, whispering in our ear, "I love you…I created you…please come and sit at my dinner table, so we can converse and engage in a beautiful relationship together along with my Son who sacrificed everything for our relationship with you."

In the garden of Gethsemane, Jesus surrendered it all for you and me. The least we can do is surrender it all to him. For his love is deeper and wider and higher than we can possibly imagine.

> Command those who are rich in this present world not to be arrogant nor to put their hope in wealth, which is so uncertain, but to put their hope in God, who richly provides us with everything for our enjoyment. Command them to do good, to be rich in good deeds, and to be generous and willing to share. In this way they will lay up treasure for themselves as a firm foundation for the coming age, so that they may take hold of the life that is truly life. (Paul, 1 Timothy 6:17–19)

"So that they may take hold of the life that is truly life." This, this right here is what it is all about. These words, this book and all that it entails, has been orchestrated by God himself. I may have had a small part, and I know there is a lot of my own personal struggles and challenges embedded in this book, but that is the cool part, as I write it, God is working on it. I am just a man who loves Jesus passionately and is hoping to bring the love and light of Jesus into the world around me.

So after all of the evidence, after all of the debates, after all that that I have brought to the table, it is imperative that we open our eyes to see so clearly in this world of absolute evil, the death, the murder, abortion, war, greed, extreme sexual perversion, absolute confusion, corrupt governments all over the world, child trafficking, mental illness, extreme drug and alcohol addiction, extreme pornography, wars and rumors of wars, climate calamities—our world is sinking into the darkest and most evil time in our history, the world is collapsing all around us and is only falling deeper and deeper into the clutches of the evil one; it is so clearly obvious then, we are entering into the last days. There is no greater time than now to take account of all that is happening in our world to become *aware* of that which is coming to pass, the prophecies of old. If this doesn't *wake you up*, then nothing will. Until the time comes when those who choose not to listen will be left behind to then live with the consequences of their choices and actions. And if you are left behind, this will be the most terrifying times in the history of mankind. Please do not be deciding that this is a scare tactic, it is not; it is absolutely real, and it is happening…*now*. The endgame is near. And you have been warned. God is trying to reach you. He is calling to you to turn your face to God now and seek out his Son, Jesus. Please, this is not something you want to toy with. I urge you today, get right with God.

Please allow me to pray with you these words (read them aloud so he may wash over you): Lord Jesus, we pray Lord that these words, these Holy Spirit moments will penetrate the hearts of the people reading this book. Father, we pray that you bless their journey and along the way. May you blow their mind and heart wide open to the beauty of your love, your forgiveness, and that these beautiful and loved people would surrender it all for the kingdom! May they experience the depths of your love to their very core, and may they hear your voice while they seek you out. May God's Word penetrate our doubts, and may Jesus reveal to us the absolute beauty of his truth and worthiness to be praised. May Jesus shine his light upon us, crack open the curtain to reveal the genuineness of his glorified reality and that he may give us his peace. May we come home to be with you, Lord Jesus, in heaven forever. Amen.

May God be the glory! Amen and amen!

> Grace is when God gives us good things that we don't deserve. Mercy is when He spares us from bad things we deserve. Blessings are when He is generous with both. Truly, we can never run out of reasons to thank Him. God is Good…All…The…Time! (Pastor Greg Locke)

> And we urge you, brothers, warn those who are idle, encourage the timid, help the weak, be patient with everyone. Make sure that nobody

pays back wrong for wrong, but always try to be kind to each other and to everyone else.

Be joyful always; pray continually; give thanks in all circumstances, for this is God's will for you in Christ Jesus.

Do not put out the Spirit's fire; do not treat prophecies with contempt. Test everything. Hold on to the good. Avoid every kind of evil. May God Himself, the God of peace, sanctify you through and through. May your whole spirit, soul and body be kept blameless at the coming of our Lord Jesus Christ. The one who calls you is faithful, and He will do it. (Paul, 1 Thessalonians 5:14–24)

A Bible that is falling apart usually belongs to somebody who isn't. (Charles Spurgeon)

However, I consider my life worth nothing to me, if only I may finish the race and complete the task the Lord Jesus has given me—the task of testifying to the gospel of God's grace. (Paul, Acts 20:24)

Amen and Hallelujah!

At that time, they will see the Son of Man coming in a cloud with power and great glory. When these things begin to take place, stand up and lift up your heads, because your redemption is drawing near. (Jesus, Luke 21:27–28)

My prayer is that when I die, all of hell rejoices that… I am out of the fight. (C. S. Lewis)

SURRENDER

Therefore be careful how you walk, not as unwise men but as wise, making the most of your time, because the days are evil.

So then do not be foolish, but understand what the will of the Lord is. (Paul, Ephesians 5:15–17)

The Man in the Glass

When you get what you want in your struggle for self, and the world makes you a king for a day.

Then go to the mirror and look at yourself, and see what the man has to say.

For it isn't a man's father, mother or wife, whose judgement upon him must pass, the fellow whose verdict counts most in life, is the man staring back in the glass.

He's the fellow to please, never mind all the rest, for he's with you clear to the end.

And you've passed your most dangerous, difficult test, if the man in the glass is your friend.

You can fool the whole world down the pathway of years, and get pats on the back as you pass.

But the final reward will be heartache and tears, if you've cheated the man in the glass. (Peter Dale Wimbrow Sr.)

ABOUT THE AUTHOR

Don Baunsgard lives in Snoqualmie, Washington, with his wife, Lena, and four kids. In 2021, Don and Lena opened a nonprofit thrift store called Treasures in Heaven that accepts a wide variety of donations, ranging from household items to collectibles and antiques. When Don is not writing books, he runs the thrift store with his wife, which keeps them very busy as well as raising two teenage boys. Don's other books include the following:

- *This Thing Called Life*
- *I Bring You Good News*
- *Faithfully*

Printed in the USA
CPSIA information can be obtained
at www.ICGtesting.com
LVHW010300200724
785213LV00009B/2